Manoj Das and Laxmi's Adventure

Manoj Das and Laxmi's Adventure

Prof. Manindra Kumar Meher

Translated by
Ipsita Das

BLACK EAGLE BOOKS
Dublin, USA | Bhubaneswar, India

Black Eagle Books
USA address:
7464 Wisdom Lane
Dublin, OH 43016

India address:
E/312, Trident Galaxy, Kalinga Nagar,
Bhubaneswar-751003, Odisha, India

E-mail: info@blackeaglebooks.org
Website: www.blackeaglebooks.org

First International Edition Published by
Black Eagle Books, 2023

MANOJ DAS AND LAXMI'S ADVENTURE
by **Prof. Manindra Kumar Meher**
Translated by **Ipsita Das**

Original Copyright © Prof. Manindra Kumar Meher
Translation Copyright © Ipsita Das

All rights reserved. No part of this publication may be reproduced, stored in a retrieval system, or transmitted, in any form or by any means, electronic, mechanical, photocopying, recording or otherwise without the prior permission of the publisher.

Cover & Interior Design: Ezy's Publication

ISBN- 978-1-64560-379-5 (Paperback)
Library of Congress Control Number: 2023936042

Printed in the United States of America

On the occasion of English edition

I am greatly inspired by Manoj Das's story 'Laxmi's Adventure'. The readers have definitely got the idea of how much it touched my heart. Manoj Das is a great national and international writer. That is why, I sincerely want the English version of this book to be published. I am very happy that Ipsita Das, who is my colleague as well as a younger sister to me and also an assistant professor of English in the P. G. Department of Language and Literature shows her interest in translating this book into English. As a writer I gave a suggestion to her to translate the book in simple English which will be heart touching for all the readers. The English readers of this book can measure its value. I will feel blessed when the book is picked up by the literature lovers of the great writer Manoj Das. On this occasion, I express my sincere thanks to the translator Ipsita Das. I am deeply grateful to the Black Eagle Books, USA for accepting the responsibility of publishing the book.

I will get real satisfaction if the book is accepted by the readers.

Manindra Kumar Meher

On behalf of the translator

Being a student and faculty of English literature, how can I forget Manoj Das! All of his stories are my favourite. The influence of the story 'Laxmi's Adventure' is very deep on me. I felt really happy when I got the opportunity to read the book 'Laxmi's Adventure' written by senior professor of our department Prof. Manindra Kumar Meher. I never thought of a book composition based on a single short story. After reading the book, I realised its importance. I am feeling blessed after getting the opportunity to translate it into English. The true judges of how well the book has been translated are the readers and the critics. I have simply translated it in my own style. If the readers are able to understand the book, it will be a great happiness for me.

Ipsita Das
Translator

CONTENTS

A Letter for Laxmi	11
The image of a painful soul: Laxmi's father	14
All over the World: Laxmi's Mother	17
Confessions of the priest in the story 'Laxmi's Adventure'	21
Prayer by the Soul of the pond	24
The best works of fiction: 'Laxmi's Adventure'	28
The little girl's condition is more important than two bananas	32
The greatness of the money lender	36
The great mercy of Laxmikant	39
Manoj Das's Popular story 'Laxmi's Adventure'	43
Laxmi is the conscious counterpart of Savitri	47
Gangadhar's Sita and Manoj's Laxmi	50
Two feverish characters: a divine woman and a regretted child	53
Conversation of Laxmi and God	56
Manoj Das's 'Aranyaka' and 'Laxmi's Adventure': A Comparative study	60
Two rays of divine light: Rebati and Laxmi	65
Manoj Das's 'Laxmi's Adventure' and Oscar Wilde's 'The Selfish Giant' : A Comparative study	68
An expression of the desire of divine Mother: 'Laxmi's Adventure' and 'Nivedita ra Naishavisara'	73
'The Letter of the Last Spring' and 'Laxmi's Adventure' : Two divine daughters	80
'Groom for Sita' and 'Laxmi's Adventure'	83
'Sarvabhuteshu' and 'Laxmi's Adventure'	87
Raibabu in 'Teeth' and the priest in 'Laxmi's Adventure'	90
The voice of compassion in 'Laxmi's Adventure'	93
The Mysterious Secret of Child Psychology: 'Laxmi's Adventure'	96
The Experience of Laxmi	100
The best story of Manoj Das	104
Two Glorious Forms of Divine Mother	108
Background	111

A Letter for Laxmi

Dear Laxmi,

Those who have read 'Laxmi's Adventure' by Manoj Das, a well-known writer of Odisha and all over India, have kept you in their heart. 'Laxmi's Adventure' is one of the famous stories of Manoj Das. The way you have been portrayed in this story makes everyone emotional. How pure, how beautiful, how innocent is your heart! Just as you can talk to God in your dreams, so you can come and meet him in the temple when the priest is asleep in the daytime. You brought two bananas from God. In that incident the Priest accused you of theft, and you entered the pond up to your waist in fear. Your father came and rescued you from there. But you remained completely speechless. After three days, you left the world. When people prayed to God after getting the proof of his existence, the priest, who accused you of theft, realised at that moment that God left the throne. All that remains is a lightless and meaningless form. The priest prayed in fever before his death, 'Lord, in the next birth, this sin man may be born tongueless.'

Whoever reads this heart touching book will never forget you. I have also read the story. The way Manoj Das has described about the Priest's change of heart, is deeply felt by the readers. The writer has felt that the real beauty of the soul is hidden in a man, no matter how cruel he is. The way you have dedicated your life to raise the soul of human beings, I always wonder who you are? Is it possible to find an answer to such questions easily? But with God's mercy, the impossible becomes possible. Divine mother is rising on your face when we slowly look at you. Manoj Das has discovered the great feeling of motherhood in every little girl. But, O Goddess, O Sri maa, you appeared in the form of a little girl and spontaneously came to life in Manoj's writings. Goddess, your mercy is infinite. You have come down to this earth to transform all human cruelty into modesty.

I am reminded of the great novelist Oscar Wilde's story 'The Selfish Giant' . The cruel protagonist has a beautiful garden but he does not allow the children to play in it. The spring doesn't come to that garden when the children are banned from entering it. After many days, that selfish man hears the sound of sweet music and is startled by the fragrance of the flowers. He comes out of the house and sees the children are playing in the garden by jumping the wall. After the entrance of the children into the garden, the trees become flowery. In that auspicious moment, there is no cruelty in the heart of that selfish man. His heart fills with love. He feels that the flowers were certainly beautiful, but the most beautiful of all are the children. Seeing a little child, he feels immense joy. Seeing that child after many days, his joy knows no bounds; But what is this! The little child has injuries on his hands and feet. The man asks about the reason for his injury and the little boy says it is wound of love. The child says again he will take the man to his own garden, if he will allow him to play there. After reading the story and imagining this little child, one can often be reminded of Jesus Christ. In order to spread love in the cruel men's heart, Jesus Christ came down in the form of a child through the writings of Oscar Wilde to this world. My Laxmi is like this. You are no one else, you are the Divine mother of Pondicherry monastery. To change the arrogant hearts of human beings, you have descended to this earth. Mother, I bow down to you and also to Manoj, the great creator of that great consciousness through which you are revealed.

The image of a painful soul: Laxmi's father

It is not easy to free the character's painful heart in literature. One such character is Laxmi's father in the story 'Laxmi's Adventure'. Laxmi's heart fills with deep respect, devotion, sympathy and affection for her loving father. Laxmi is praying to God for her father's well-being, like a mother, just as her father did for her. She is requesting God to arrange some money for her father. One day, when she expresses her desire to buy a new frock, her father says to her mother, "My daughter never asks for anything - today I will buy a new frock for her." In these words, Laxmi's personality appears and she also expresses her immense love and respect for her father. Laxmi describes before God about the incident that happened on that day. Her voice is softening when she says, "After a long time, she (her mother) came out from home with me and my father - to buy a frock for me and to walk around. God! We have just left the house, and a fat, snotty man came. Father took as much money as he had and gave it to that man. Father borrowed some money from him. After seven days, that terrible man came with a big stick and took the interest money. Father said that the person has already taken one and half the interest of the money he gave. Shouldn't he be satisfied with that?"

When we look at the life of the great writer Manoj Das, we say that he was first attracted towards Marxism and eventually became successful in the philosophy of Sri Aurobindo. But did the idea of Marxism completely disappear from him? No, that cannot be said at all. Here, in the conversation of Laxmi with God, one hears the awe inspiring voice of Manoj, who expresses his sympathy in the sufferings of men. Here Laxmi's father is representing the exploited class. The lamentation of this exploited soul, which touched Manoj's heart with empathy, is becoming soulful in Laxmi's song. Is this just an expression of Laxmi's soul? Manoj is directly asking questions to the exploiting class- "Shouldn't they be satisfied with that?" Here, the pulse of Marxist thought, Gandhi's call of conscience, Vivekananda's call to heart - everything is mirrored. Can we get the final conclusion after seeing the picture that Manoj was fond of from the beginning?

After that the tremor created in the heart of Laxmi's father, neither Manoj has the ability to write it, nor the readers have to read it. The scene of Laxmi's father shedding tears in the middle of the story can make any reader's heart skip a beat.

The readers again see Laxmi's father in the story. When Laxmi enters the pond in fear of the priest and people along with him look at her with red eyes to come out of the pond, then Laxmi's father comes out towards the pond by pushing the crowd. Laxmi is crying as soon as she sees her father. Stepping into the water, the father picks her up in his arms. This is all about Laxmi's father. He brings Laxmi from the pond to give her a new life, when the life lamp of Laxmi extinguishes prematurely, he carries her in his arms to the graveyard by making his heart a stone. Perhaps there is no need to raise this compassionate scene in the story. Does the definition of a short story sound familiar? Therefore, the inability of his soul to provide such a picture is implied in the narrative. The unexpressed sorrows and tears of Laxmi's father can reach the soul of those who feel and suffer.

Laxmi's father has nothing but one sentence on his face. That is 'My daughter never asks for anything, today I will buy her a new frock.' Ah, this sentence shakes the earth. All the compassion of a father is in this sentence. This sentence is not in one father's heart, but in a million fathers' heart. So there is no need to explain more. In literature, such characters emerge, who are the constant idols of silence. They say nothing. The readers feel every beat of their heart and every cell of their blood. Laxmi's father is a great example of divine love. Laxmi is his divine daughter. Laxmi is his mother. There is no way to stop the tears of a father who has lost his little daughter forever. It is natural for the readers to consider the author's emotion because that compassionate feeling is unexpressed. A reader may not consciously know that Laxmi's heart is constantly crying like her father. There are also the tears of Laxmi's mother. The writer's soul is also the same as their inner soul. Our patience has not yet been broken by not placing it in the story. The author of this book apologises to everyone for the great sin of breaking that infinite patience.

All over the World: Laxmi's Mother

This idea of Laxmi's Mother is not the researcher's opinion. The words written in the text for her mother are the words of Laxmi, the main character of the story.

The image of Laxmi's mother remains unchanged in the hearts of those who have studied the story 'Laxmi's Adventure'. There is no special mention of Laxmi's mother in the story. The two or three sentences in her conversation reveal the characteristics of her motherly heart. Laxmi, like every child, expects an answer from her mother to the question raised in her mind. In the temple, Laxmi expresses her heart to God. In that, she says, "Dear God, Can you hear the prayer through the instruments?" One day she asks the same to her mother. She Says, "Dear mother, did Dhruva Prahallad used to pray to God with the help of instruments?" After thinking for a while mother says "no". Mother always says the right thing, doesn't she? Laxmi expresses her opinion about her mother through this question. The answers to the questions that arise in every child's heart are given by the mother. Mother's expression leaves a deep impression in a child's mind. It remains clear in their heart with the passing of the time. Laxmi's mother is a compassionate being with inner consciousness. Whatever she says to Laxmi from the depth of her heart creates empathy in the reader's. The simplicity of Laxmi's heart, which disturbs the reader, has actually come from the inner soul of her mother. Laxmi is as pure, as beautiful, as devoted as her mother, there is no doubt. Mother heartily loves Laxmi. She wants to keep her happy despite all the family problems. One day when Laxmi wants to buy a frock and she cannot afford it for the cruel man who takes money from her father, she says to her mother "Dear mother, your old saree has been in the box since days. You never use it. You will sew a frock for me from that saree, there is no need for market frocks." The sentence that Laxmi tells, she knows that it is a lie. She says this because she doesn't want not to hurt her mother's heart. But Laxmi knows the ability to gain sensitivity to her mother's pain, there is no doubt. While mother is sewing a frock from her saree in the evening, Laxmi notices that she is crying. Once again, she notices the tears in mother's eyes. When the terrible man comes to his father to take interest money, that day her mother lies to that man. For self-defence, she says that Laxmi's father has gone far away, he will return after seven days. Mother has always inspired Laxmi to speak the truth. When she lies, Laxmi says to her, "You said that lying is bad - how did you say it?" After listening to this question, her mother's answer is filled with immense pain. She says, "Lying is bad, I said it because I am in trouble." Then she brings Laxmi into her arms and says very intimately, "But you will be a better human being than me. You will never tell a lie even if you are in trouble." After listening mother's words, Laxmi notices that mother is hiding her tears. Laxmi feels that her mother may have lied to her, but she is not a liar. "She is all over the whole world."

  This great experience of Laxmi is really heart touching. Every child's holy soul thinks his mother is the best truth. In fact, everything that Laxmi experiences is above the whole earth, she also receives strength from her mother.

Her mother is a great combination of sensitivity, devotional sentiments, consciousness, compassion and generosity. All these qualities are also in Laxmi. The child, whose mother is great, never falls into the lower consciousness. Laxmi's mother is not just an ordinary woman giving love. To her Laxmi is a goddess of beauty. Mother must have felt the truth in her heart that Laxmi is not an ordinary girl. She is the glorious ray of Goddess Laxmi. There is no need for her to reveal these things. Here there is no need to explain it more because what has not been explained, the great truth is clearly revealed in the mother's sentence of the story. It is only a matter of feeling that Laxmi's mother is a loving mother and considers her not only as her own child, but as an immortal being on earth embodied in a divine soul.

Let us focus for a moment on the childhood of Sri maa in Pondicherry. She was born in France. When she was only five years old, she often thought while sitting in a small chair. Her mother once asked her, - "You are sitting like holding the thought of the whole world is in your head." In response to this, Sri maa said, "Yes maa, you are right." I am overwhelmed by all the world." The reason for mentioning this is that Sri maa's mother might not be aware of her divine appearance on that day. That is why we can here compare Sri maa's mother with Laxmi's mother. Sri maa's mother is revealed in a new form in this story. If Laxmi is Sri maa's divine consort, her mother should be the mother of Sri maa. That is why motherhood has been portrayed by the writer Manoj Das in a rare and noble form. This is not being dragged here. In this regard, Manoj has consciously commented that this is not even possible. Manoj is only a medium, a base. Just as Sri maa herself appears in the form of Laxmi through his writings, similarly, the subtle essence of her mother becomes available in the form of Laxmi's mother. Here is the ending of all the previous births. On that day Sri maa's mother was not conscious about the secret appearance of Sri maa, but now she is a conscious mother in 'Laxmi's Adventure' story.

When Laxmi talks to God and returns after three days to the world from which she came, there is no picture of Laxmi's mother portrayed here. It could not have been drawn. It would not have been appropriate. In Laxmi's absence, we cannot imagine the appearance of her mother. On the one hand, as a mundane mother, she must have been deeply grieved, and on the other hand, as an enlightened mother, she must have deeply felt that her child is born with a special purpose. After that purpose is accomplished, the deity returns to her divine world. There is no need to explain this about Laxmi's mother. It is not available to us in the essence of a story. We can have a proper vision of Laxmi and become aware of the greatness of her mother. Undoubtedly, it is remarkable to see how deep this awareness will take us into the poetic beauty of Laxmi and her mother and how many closed doors will be opened in our hearts. Without describing anything else, in Laxmi's language, it is enough to say that her mother is 'she is all over the whole world'.

Confessions of the priest in the story "Laxmi's Adventure"

You all know that 'Laxmi's Adventure' story is one of the best stories of the famous writer Manoj Das. In this story, you have seen my cruel behaviour towards the innocent little girl Laxmi and you must have looked at me with hatred. In fact, I did not know that the girl Laxmi was an idol. She was a moving Goddess. I did not have the courage to access the relationship she had with God in the temple. That's why often I use my harsh voice for her, for which she couldn't come inside the temple. I did not get a chance to enter the temple and listen to the conversation she had with God because I was taking a rest on the temple porch in the afternoon. I fell asleep, that is my consciousness remained asleep. Falling asleep in the afternoon indicates my unconsciousness. Manoj Das understood that stupidity in me. When I woke up, I saw Laxmi coming out of the temple with two bananas in her hand. Thinking about how this little girl brought two bananas from the temple, I got angry at her. Did I know that God himself gave her a double gift of those bananas? Stupid man like me ran after her by calling her a thief and made many people gather there. People like me remained in the darkness of ignorance. They supported me and accused the girl. The most important thing is the girl's character which is my ignorance. The little girl entered the pond with fear of me and the people. After some time her father came and rescued her from there. This incident created a superstition in the minds of the people that the God of temple is the direct deity. I thought, She would not survive because she had entered the temple and taken bananas. Laxmi suffered from fever. Two or three days later, she died prematurely. That time was the best moment of my life. Because at that moment I suddenly felt feverish and realised that I had committed a crime. That's why I spent the remaining few days praying to God to make me speechless in my next birth. You have heard my prayer, that's why your hearts have been kind towards me. Seeing my change, some people were surprised and asked the creator of my character, Manoj Das, why did I change so much? Manoj replied that 'no matter how bad a person is, the spirit within him must be revealed one day.' My creator's answer is literally true. That day I realised that I have a sensitive soul.

But I have not expressed the reason for writing this confession. I have to tell myself that this is not the end of the matter. Even my author Manoj Das did not explain that point, so today I have to explain it. Do you know what that secret is? That is Laxmi, the true Goddess and I feel that she had landed on this earth and died after the change of my character. It may be true that God had left the temple. But there is another deep secret in it. In that moment, I also felt another truth that - God left the idol then in a moment he entered into me as a ray of light. That's why I suffered and repent for that. It was God who entered into me and spoke to me, soothed my heart and gave me a great rebirth before I breathed my last. This rebirth gave me a chance to live on earth for a while. It was because of that I came to this earth. I have worshipped God for years, but God never entered into me. That's why my mouth was filled with harsh words and my behaviour was filled with cruelty. When God showered mercy on me, the heart of a character like me was broken. My heart became the temple of God. The auspicious sound I heard inside that temple was something I had never heard before. If God himself had not entered into me with compassion, how could I have uttered the words which the author has written. It was God who again entered himself in the heart of Manoj Das and transformed My character alive through his writings. Today I am overwhelmed with gratitude to my Lord, to my mother Laxmi, to the talented writer Manoj Das who shaped my character. I am also eternally grateful to the readers who witnessed my transformation. May God enter into the hearts of those readers who are spiritually weak like me so that man will be possessed by the divine spirit. If you have ever shown the slightest cruelty to anyone, let the tears of remorse melt your heart. Your heart may become the throne of God. You all have seen the scene of my Lord leaving the throne. The scene that remained behind the screens needs to be revealed here. A man who has been touched by divine mercy like me, is reborn. A cruel and harsh heart becomes soft and compassionate. It was the greatest experience of my life that the lotus blossomed in the mud of my heart. Experiences which I could not acquire throughout my life were made available in a single moment by the touch of his infinite grace. I have nothing to say. I humbly expressed this as I felt that it was only my duty to express. Does my creator Manoj Das do not know this matter ! He knows everything. Everything cannot be explained. Ironically, my creator reveals the divine truth. That's why I am eternally grateful to him like the readers. It is my deep hope and faith that my humble confession will never displease Manoj Das. Rather, he must feel supreme satisfaction by divine experience.

Prayer by the Soul of the pond

I am that pond into which the frightened Laxmi entered. When a pond was dug here and it was filled with rain, that was the turning point of my life. This pond is dedicated for the service of the people in the village. I was taking great pleasure in this dedication. Hundreds of people have bathed in my water over the years. I feel satisfied and grateful when people bathe in my water. I knew that a deep longing existed in each of my water as Laxmi walked through this path. Ah! What a beautiful name Laxmi is! What a soft girl she is! What is the simplicity around her, what is the light of love! As soon as I saw her, every part of my body trembled. In my mind, I was thinking that if this divinely beautiful girl entered my soul, I would get a unique joy.

I spent each day waiting for Laxmi. I was praying to God to give me a chance to hug Laxmi once. That day, when Laxmi came to the temple in the afternoon, I was looking at her with a smile on my face. At that time, I felt that I could be closer to God's mercy. I could not find the reason why it seemed like this. But after some time, she started running out of the temple, I saw the priest chasing after her with a harsh shout. I was shocked and stared at her. How do I know that at that moment my years of waiting will be complete! Laxmi jumped into me like a baby jumps into his mother's arms. I can think of nothing for a moment. When

Laxmi entered into my soul, all my longing water drops were satisfied as they were waiting for her for years. Her breath was very heavy. I was clinging to Laxmi. She stands in my water. At that time. I was anxious to give her love. I grabbed her. I gave her so many loving kisses. I could not know whether it was the sound of pain or joy when the birds swarmed in my water. They must be happy with Laxmi. But I could not understand that they were in great pain by looking at her scared face.

I can't find the words to explain the feeling when Laxmi was residing in my heart. The priest was shouting at the shore, he could never dare to come to the pond. At that moment I realised that Laxmi was a goddess. The supernatural beings cannot approach her at all. That is why no one could enter into me. When Laxmi's father came, I welcomed him warmly. He was fit to enter the pond. Because he had a clear heart. I was glorified by the touch of his heart. When Laxmi's father took Laxmi in his arms, I was shocked to see this loving union of father and daughter. I thought that the touch of both of them made me double sacred. I thought to myself that if I could get the chance to hug these two father and daughter together every day, then I would feel like heaven. This feeling will remain in my mind forever - how do I know this! Later I heard Laxmi's suffering from fever. And heard that her soul had left her body and flown towards the sky. Who could have seen the tears I filled in my body! I thought that the coldness in me made Laxmi leave her body! I cursed myself for thinking how miserable I was. Just then the soul of Laxmi floated in the waves of the wind and said to me - 'I am sacrificing my life not for you, but for the priest.' I understood the secret of everything from this one sentence.

She was not just an ordinary girl. She was a great part of the divine. The Goddess Laxmi. I could feel myself sanctified by her touch. From that day I did not consider myself unlucky but rather considered lucky. I realised that Laxmi has made a difference in my life by giving the place of mother.

You know what happened next. The change in the priest proved that Laxmi was the heavenly goddess and had come down to earth with a great purpose.

I humbly reveal to you the fact that no one knows and it is not mentioned in the story. I was just a small village pond. But you will be surprised to know how the people of the village honoured me from that day. From that day on, I was no longer an ordinary pond. My name became 'Laxmi-Sagar'. I have already said that I am a small pond. Where is the vast ocean and where is the small body of water like me! This comparison seems unreal. But I received this great name as I got the sacred touch of Laxmi.

Hundreds of people bathe in my water every year to commemorate the anniversary of Laxmi and my great union. If you bathe in my water on this particular day, all your sins will be washed away. Since that day, I have been immersed in everyone's mind with the feeling of a holy ocean. To that great Goddess Laxmi, I pray that you come down to the bosom of the earth. By your touch, neglected ponds like me would gain the glory of the sea. But if you come again, dear Laxmi mother, I will not let you go again. I will hold you forever in my heart. I never imagined that such a prayer would reach this great goddess. Every day at noon, when the environment is quiet and still, then the subtle light of Mother Laxmi emerges and enters me, gives me immense comfort. I embrace my beloved mother and get divine blessings whenever I am alone. That's why my water is never contaminated. I am like Ganga of this village. I am like the ocean of the Sri Jagannath temple. My whole life has been blessed. You are great, mother. Thank you for your mercy, and we got immense glory by receiving the rays of this mercy.

I can't finish speaking the words of my heart. Even the prayers in my heart are unfinished. I am eternally grateful to the one who has given me the strength to bless my life by donating water. I do not have the ability to express this gratitude. I am only holding this eternal mother in every drop of my water and praying to her throughout the day and night.

The best works of fiction: 'Laxmi's Adventure'

'Laxmi's Adventure' is one of the best works of fiction. But the art of story doesn't just explain the exterior part. It is a heart-warming expression of an inherent art. If someone could have composed a story by studying the definition, then the best story would have been composed effortlessly even by many critics. Even it is not possible to compose a story when one is only aware of the features of the story. The art of story composition needs to be aware of its inner aspects, as well as its outward appearance.

Those who compose stories for the reader's pleasure, it may be pleasant to read, but it doesn't touch the heart always. It is not easy to express in general the artistry of the writers who only write for the pleasure of mankind.

The beginning of the story must be suspenseful, it must be moral rather than descriptive, the morals of the story must not be directly presented, the story must contain a single idea and the ending must be able to fill the reader with satisfaction - all these beauties must bloom in the story. It is very difficult to say about the size of the story beforehand. Before writing a short story one must read the poem 'Barsajapana' by Rabindranath Tagore. Rabindranath himself has written short stories, and has violated many rules. Because when the fire of inspiration emerges in the soul, then all the principles burn in it and become into ashes. By this, the structural beauty is not disturbed, but the analysis is sharpened and a new life is created in the reader's heart.

In both physical and spiritual achievements, the success of 'Laxmi's Adventure' is unimaginable. But is it really possible to distinguish between the structure and elements of the story? It is quite normal for the soul to shine within the body. In every sentence of the story 'Laxmi's Adventure', the reader can notice the style of presentation and word connection. Is it possible to plan and describe how a story starts, how it will develop and how it will end? It is a rare experience to see how the story comes to the mind of the writer. Even the writer himself doesn't know how the words, characters, scenes are drawn by him, which he does not think about. The story 'Laxmi's Adventure' was not a product of Manoj's planned imagination. This is a reflection of his soul. Sri maa from Pondicherry has highlighted the sincerity of telling a beautiful story. In it, she states that those who truly possess a creative spirit tell a mystical story that inspires hope. Looking at it from this point of view, we can easily realise that Manoj is a great story-writer.

The way Laxmi appears before the readers at the beginning of the story is definitely a source of anxiety for the readers. Her exchange of thought with God is very simple. At the end the pride of the Priest turns into his repentance. But it is a mystery that Manoj creates a new thought wave in his mind and describes it in his pen. To Unveil this mystery is impossible. It is the source for him, who knows how to make the story beautiful. Those who enter the spiritual sanctum of their art - their vision is different from ordinary writers. This can be deeply felt while reading the story 'Laxmi's Adventure'. Sri maa also answered many questions about the mysterious relationship between art and spirituality. This demonstrates the importance of how spiritual inspiration can settle a writer's intuition. In the opinion of many, the compositions of the spiritual writer are often in danger. But the spirituality that Sri maa is highlighting, it never ends the artistic creation. Rather, this art can be spiritually illuminated, artistically refined and inspirational. If there is a flow of divine grace in the story, it lifts the reader's soul to a higher place.

Every character described in the story seems so true, so realistic, so close that the reader forgets that it is a story. In fact, 'Laxmi's Adventure' is not just a fictional story. That is the great power which can express a great truth. The reason why the story has enlightened the hearts of readers over the years is that it is a great creation. That is the art, which makes life-art blossom. There is no difference between fiction and spirituality. The rays of real spirituality reflect in the fine art. 'Laxmi's Adventure' is the successful writing of a great artist which is the best example to show how art for art and art for life can be distinguished.

Critics who are saying Oscar Wilde, the great literary sculptor of the Western world, as an artist of Art for Art's sake, fail to realise how the sublime beauty of morality shines in his short stories. We fail to establish the merits of such authors by including them in any group . On the other hand, it is a heart-warming expression to realise how unique is the fiction, art and ethics of such a highly conscious writer. The issue of morality that is raised here is far above social morality. That is the closest thing to spirituality. Manoj's presentation of talent in fiction has impressed both English and Odia readers. 'Laxmi's Adventure' is a clear appreciation of the infinite beauty expressed in his art and it shows how sacred and pure the story is.

The little girl's condition is more important than two bananas

The little girl's condition is more important than two bananas. This is the language of the heartless crowd who have mixed their own voice with the voice of the priest. When Laxmi enters into the pond to escape from the priest's anger, the readers are shocked by the presence of the heartless crowd. These merciless people are responsible for Jesus Christ's crucifixion. It is these people who forced Socrates to drink poison. And these are the people who shot Mahatma Gandhi in the chest. Laxmi is half drowned in that pool and dripped blood like Jesus. Like Socrates, she is silent while drinking the noise of the poisonous words of the ignorant crowd. The words coming out of each one's mouth is piercing her chest and the blood is flowing from her inner soul.

Just as the cruel father had tried to push the devotee Prahallad to death, the same effort is in these people. Human beings are always agitated by the simple passion of devotion. They are constantly anxious for the salvation of the souls, killing themselves by joining hands with the blind masses. Those who have sacrificed their lives like Laxmi, are not worthy in the eyes of the public and in the eyes of a powerful ruler. Ah ! Have these people received the commandment from God to describe the character of these great souls ! Sri maa has warned us not to bother anyone. People don't really have the ability to give fame to others. It is impossible to judge the humanity of those who are pointing fingers at Laxmi's character with the priest's loud voice on that day! They are not able to realise the existence of God. Who are they to give an opinion on Laxmi? They know how to kill characters. The power of building characters, to describe the greatness in characters are not aroused in them. That is why existentialist writers and philosophers call them 'bad people'. In other words, these groups are even lower than animals without conscience. They are as ignorant as shelled almonds. They have shown their ignorance in all ages in determining the differences between the good, the bad, the beautiful and the ugly. How can we expect a sweet word for Laxmi from these ignorant, fearless, cruel crowds?

In the story 'Laxmi's Adventure', writer Manoj has pictured the merciless crowd in two scenes. One is in the above nonsense and the another is that after the death of Laxmi, when the voice of 'Haribol' comes out from blind crowd saying God is the direct deity. They do not have even the slightest love or sympathy for the girl. No one shed tears on the death of Laxmi. Did the people get the proof that whoever has taken bananas from the temple cannot be saved? What else could be expected from this ignorant and merciless crowd? They see only external events. They are eternally deprived from the touch of the divinity hidden in the events. For this, God casts a sad eye on this merciless crowd. God died in the form of Laxmi to kindle the lamp of knowledge in the ignorant people, to open the true eyes of the blind, and to create a little love in the merciless men.

This story is a great lesson for the people to remove

the veil of darkness that covers the hearts of the ignorant people. Manoj's writings are only a means to give this divine sign. Using Manoj's extraordinary talent, God has given the readers a message of consciousness, which is very useful in their daily life. After reading such a story, the blind eyes of ignorant people will be opened one by one. After reciting it, the doors of the heart will be opened. The lamp that has been extinguished in the soul of the people will soon be enlightened. In this way the blind people will gradually gain the true power of vision. All will learn how to love, forgive and bless others. When Sri Aurobindo was imprisoned, he saw God there. God was also seen between the lawyers who were arguing. The man who was sitting on the judge seat looked like the beloved God Sri Krishna. Therefore, we can imagine how these ignorant people look in the eyes of the great God. It will never be justified to say that maa Laxmi has forgiven them all, she has rained her blessings to open their inner eyes. There is no description of this in any sentence of the story. There is no need to explain. This truth cannot be expressed in words. It is expressed in silence. It is unwritten. It is unheard. Only they, whose inner door is open, can hear the sweet voice of the divine mother.

The story portrays the character of a cruel man, who transforms into a good human being. The writer is not satirising such people in the story, because satire alone does not change anyone forever. That's why God has showered his unconditional love on the people. When the soul of the priest is realising, then the question will rise up in the crowd to think it is the death of Laxmi or the death of the priest. Those who have an idea in this aspect must have felt the appearance and disappearance of Laxmi. They have also understood the inner truth that is revealed in the death of the priest. This compassion of mother Laxmi is only a symbolic expression given to bring reconciliation. This is a great attempt to open the doors of the souls of people. Manoj is blessed for playing this great role and people are also blessed who are able to see the truth by reading it

Therefore, the abundance of motherly compassion in the story can give the readers such an infinite power by which they can gain their consciousness.

The greatness of the money lender

You all know about the cruelty of my character. It is also known to everyone how I forcefully extorted loan interest from Laxmi's father. Laxmi's father took a loan from me. That is why it was my duty to collect interest from him every month. These poor people borrow money, but cannot repay it on time. For this my anger rises. So, I approach them without delay to collect interest money. In the same way or because of that habit, I took away the interest money from Laxmi's father. That's it. I had no interest in knowing what happened next.

Did I know that the famous writer of Odisha will write a story by centering this little girl Laxmi! There was no chance for this story to gain my attention. But when I heard the story from the gentlemen, I came to know that the money I forcibly took away from Laxmi's father, that amount was to buy a new frock for her. For that, Laxmi with her parents went to buy a frock but at that time very cruelly I took away that money. Later I came to know that when Laxmi entered the temple and prayed, she requested her father not to borrow money from people like me.

The next month, when I went to Laxmi's house to collect the interest money, I heard the sad story of her life. How the priest had chased her while stealing the temple's bananas, how Laxmi entered into the pond and how her father rescued her from there - after hearing the news of

Laxmi's sudden death, a stone hearted man like me felt that someone was crying silently inside my heart. Later, I realised that it was my evil spirit. The death of a girl like Laxmi created deep pain in the entire village. Since that day, I no longer have the courage to go to Laxmi's house to collect the interest money. I cannot think how to ask for money by looking at the faces of childless parents. After hearing the words of Manoj Das's story and listening the voice of the priest's heart from people, tears of repentance are also flowing from my heart. It is not only the priest who is responsible for the death of Laxmi. The role of an antihero like me is very vital in this story. After knowing all these, I did not dare to come out of my house. My insides are just cracking out. I don't know what my duty is. I don't even sleep at night. The innocent faces of Laxmi and her father can only be seen to my eyes. I have not the ability to address them. I don't even have the courage to stand by them.

I am only telling you to know that my stick, which created fear in Laxmi's heart, was thrown away in the pool in which Laxmi entered. I have no more stick in my hands. Now I am empty-handed, my face is down with remorse. According to the prayer that Laxmi made in front of God, my appearance has changed today. But Laxmi is no more alive to see this sympathetic face of mine. To me it is a pitiful punishment. I bear this and keep Laxmi of my heart as my own daughter with all the tears and joy of love and compassion.

The writer Manoj Das would get some rest to write all the words of my heart. The story ended with the priest's repentance, and what happened in my life after that, there is no need to describe it. I am just a flat character in this story. After all, can I forget that I am an antihero? So today, after many years of the composition of 'Laxmi's Adventure' story, I am standing before you with a very ashamed and dirty heart. You readers shouldn't forgive me. You should curse on me that I will get smaller and smaller. And you will never see my long stick. It has been dipped in Laxmi's Sea. I am also waiting for the day when I will go to Laxmi and greet her in heaven and buy a frock for her from mortal land.

The great mercy of Laxmikant

The little girl Laxmi entered the temple to see Laxmikant. He is the source of divine power. He receives the devotional offerings and satisfies with whatever is offered to him on this earth. He descended in the form of Ramachandra for Sita. He appears in the form of Sri Krishna for Sri Radha and for the other *gopis*. Goddess Laxmi takes care of him and to get that care he appears in the form of Sri Jagannath. His majesty is immense and unimaginable. When Mahabharata's Vidura offered him a banana peel instead of a banana, he accepted it with reverence. Even his mercy and love delights the devotees.

There is not even a single line of description of what this almighty Laxmikant said in this story. The fact that he called Laxmi only in her dream. He is not saying anything. He listens to Laxmi's heart with a smile on his sweet lips. The idol Laxmikant, who is silent, speaks everything in silence. In the small story, from the beginning to the end, he has expressed himself with great majesty. The readers read Laxmi's conversation with him and feel that he is answering each word of Laxmi. So, we cannot call it one sided love and care. We have no idea about the secret of what the two of them were getting from each other. Each of Laxmi's words in the temple is pronounced in such a way that Laxmi is completely merged with him. To gain this unity, he comes to the earth in various forms, in various colours, in various incarnations. Wherever he sees the spirit of love and devotion, there he remains. Wherever he sees the power of pride, he abandons it.

For this reason, after the death of Laxmi, when the crowd gives Haribol voice by portraying him as a direct deity, the author describes how he abandoned his idol. But his mercy is immense. When he sees that there is such a desire in the heart of the priest, which is directed towards the light, then he enters into him. We all know the unimaginable change that took place in the life of the priest due to his introspection.

Laxmikant has kept Laxmi's parents with his great love. The hearts of both of them were so good that he arranged a place for his beloved Laxmi to appear in their house. He knows the innermost desire of Laxmi's parents. That desire is nothing else - it is to have a divine child like Laxmi who may not live for long days but can change the world in her short lifetime. Dharmapada's parents wished the same. Ghatotkocho's mother Hidimbiki also wished to God for such a strong son. For this, God has sent his beloved Laxmi to the earth. And he also felt compassion for Laxmi's father.

Laxmikant's love for Laxmi is boundless. He shows great respect towards Laxmi's parents. And finally, his compassion is infinite even for the priest who is very cruel. When he kills Rabana in the form of Ramachandra, he pours the stream of supreme devotion towards him. He is born as the nephew of Kansa and kills him. He sucks the nectar from the poisonous breasts of Putana who came to kill him. At the end of life, he takes him to heaven. For which all call him Narayan. Even if there is a tiny hole for divine light to enter in the heart of a little life, he enters into the man with a speed faster than lightning. Even the one who hates him knows the reason by which virtue he sanctifies his life.

The stream of Laxmikanta's compassion flows unceasingly from beginning to end in the 'Laxmi's Adventure' story. He also gives his kind touch to Manoj, the author of this story. Those who read this story become holy just like those who read the Bhagavad, Vedas, and Puranas. In the same way, the heart of the man who reads this story with great determination also fills his heart in a unique way.

So the poet Gangadhar Meher is reluctant even to name Laxmikant as 'Karuna Sindhu', because Sindhu is a point of his compassion and it is impossible for humans to name God. The ability to address that compassion is also absent in human beings. In spite of all this, he is full of love and compassion, a thousand times more generous than the boundless sky. Writers like Kahlil Gibran, who says – 'It is more acceptable to say that I am in the heart of God than to say that God is in my heart.' Therefore, like the presence of the Himalaya cannot be imagined in a mustard, so the human body is unable to imagine him. Laxmikanta accepts all these great thoughts. But he is being worshipped every moment as Sitaram in Hanuman's chest. He is such a fine ray of light that no matter how small a man is, he can fix his place in it. His compassion for all is boundless. Gangadhar said - "Even though you are young, we have lived in the state of compassion / Life is in despair because of the lack of his blessings / Look at the world." As we all live within that Compassion, if we only turn a little towards him, he will shower us with infinite mercy. By drinking rainwater drop by drop like a bird, all our thirst and ignorance will be satisfied and the whole life will be revealed in indescribable divine light. The 'Laxmi's Adventure' story is only a symbol of this compassion, which is known not only in Odia literature but also in world literature.

Manoj Das's Popular story 'Laxmi's adventure'

It's not at all easy to reveal the mystery of popularity which a story gains. Even if a writer composes a hundred stories, the fame that one story gives him is really amazing. Fakir Mohan Senapati's 'Revati', Laxmikanta Mahapatra's 'Buddha Sankhari', Kalindi Charan Panigarahi's 'Mansara Bilapa', Godabarish Mahapatra's 'Magunira Shagad', these great stories of great writers estimate the way for a fictional creation to reach in readers' heart. Undoubtedly, these stories have gained popularity due to the rare qualities that exist in these which shake the heart of the readers. The innumerable creations of such great literary writers have been published and the best visions of their genius are reflected in those writings. Why and how one story can win the hearts of thousands of readers, is really unimaginable.

Manoj Das's story 'Laxmi's Adventure' is a great story as it has touched the hearts of countless readers of Odisha. Manoj is also the author of many stories. Apart from this, his other stories became popular. But the most popular among all is 'Laxmi's Adventure'.

The readers of 'Laxmi's Adventure' know very well about the content of the story. However, it would not be an exaggeration to describe the environment, characters and story as a miracle or magic that has created vibrations in the hearts of thousands of readers.

Laxmi is a little girl. No reason can ever reveal how this character of Laxmi has been established in the altar of every heart. No literary critic could have composed such powerful sentences. What is the reason behind the story that has created emotion in people? Rabindranath has poured the substance of his heart in his story 'Kabuliwala', so that it has created a sensation in the hearts of millions of readers, even after a hundred years. It is a supernatural game of God. This is the magic of a mysterious art. So the artistry in this story is expressed in many of Manoj's stories; Or the idea of this one story has spreaded an influence over the whole Odisha that can be felt by careful observation. Many critics and speakers present this story as a great example in various conferences and seminars. Again it's so amazing that while narrating the content of the story, it affects everyone's heart in such a way that even if you sit in the meeting, you can feel its waves deeply. This story is very dear to everyone. After listening to the story, the restless mind of the listeners is settled. The eyes which were devoid of thought before, now the eternal infinite sense of thought is seen in those. Even the slightest disturbance in the assembly becomes completely silent. The literature teacher who presents it to the students in the classroom may find that all students, regardless of their bad habits, listen to this story with a stunning heart. Even a small boy of seven or eight can connect with the truth of the story and knows how much more powerful it is than the magic displayed by the magician.

The subject of the story, the characters, the illustrations, the beauty of the environment, the beginning and the ending - by analysing all these, the popularity of any story cannot be discovered. Even the writer himself does not know the time of creation of the story which in the later period has strangely touched the readers hearts. Skills of the writer is not the main factor to this. How that skill turns into a mystery in this heart touching story is very important.

It is absolutely true that this story has touched everyone in a strange way. Laxmi is no longer confined to the story. She has become an intimate character in each family. For some as his sister, for some as his own daughter, for some as his beloved grand-daughter, and for some as a goddess, like this she is familiar to all. Where does such a rare energy come from? It is completely impossible to explain or analyse the idea that comes down from the inner, unknown and invisible world through which it is revealed.

However, we know that within the story lies the power that transforms one from Dasyu Ratnakar to Balmiki. It changes the evil power into the flow of divine consciousness. No one can ever deny this great truth. It cannot be counted how many strong minds have melted like wax, as the heart of the priest has been changed. Laxmi is like a lightning girl falling from the sky. Like Sita, who was born from the womb of mother earth, she is the owner of the power of the majestic goddess. She is a mother who carries a motherly heart like Yashoda. Eternal silence is within her. An indescribable certainty in her awe. The beauty of the rain floats in her eyes like clouds. The sound of someone's flute rings between her two ears. She is a mother of endurance. She shows great sympathy in forgiveness as well as compassion. Her heart is bigger and wider than the ocean. Who will understand her? Who will review it? Does anyone has the ability to show the way of how she enters into someone's heart? He is an epitome of queries. Her soul plays a supernatural role in melting the cruel heart.

Laxmi's parents are innocent like her. They smile like the petals of the flower. The priest also gets profit. Before the last breath, if divine mercy descends and transforms all violence, seeing it all will explode. Everyone's conscience will be alive, everyone's consciousness will rise. A single line, a secret prayer of hearts, penetrates thousands of hearts. It fills a hot heart with coldness. It is the sanctity of pure prayer that reveals the sight of a blind man.

Everyone has come to the earth to reach the same destination no matter which type of nature and character they are born with. For this reason, every human being searches for the way. When he sees even a tiny hole, his soul is awakened to feel the blueness of the eternal sky. It is in this one human birth, the rich experience of rebirth is attained by the grace of God. Then how much tears, how much passion, how much love, how much prayer and how much gratitude fills his heart, only he knows who sent him to the surface of the earth.

This is not a review of the reasons for the popularity of the 'Laxmi's Adventure' story. It is only a brief, incomplete glimpse of the emotional depths of the human heart. It is our fortune that we have earned the honour of being the readers of this story. There is nothing more virtuous than the life we live with the story in our hearts. The popularity of the 'Laxmi's Adventure' story remains in the reader's heart forever, this prayer spontaneously fills our soul as wide as the cloudless blue sky and full of boundless and inexpressible emotions.

Laxmi is the conscious counterpart of Savitri

Manoj Das, the famous writer of Odisha was born on 21st February 1963. In Pondicherry, when he came to the sacred place of Sri maa he felt the light of heavenly beauty appeared there in the form of 'Sri maa'. Earlier his soul had been devoted at the feet of Sri Aurobindo and Sri maa. He had no plan to live in Pondicherry. His consciousness was a great sign of his intuition and insight. His promise to his wife Samantha Devi gave a clear glimpse of his life at Sri Aurobindo Ashram, Pondicherry.

The supernatural manifestation of Sri maa in the form of Laxmi through Manoj has already been represented by this writer. When the readers try to understand the character of Laxmi from different angles today, the revelation of another intuition takes the reader to a different world.

When Manoj started living in Pondicherry, the whole atmosphere of Pondicherry was shadowed by the waves of Sri Aurobindo's intuition. Savitri is the name of the great consciousness that pervades the surroundings of Pondicherry. The vision of the 'Savitri' character by Sri Aurobindo is very clear and meaningful. So who can avoid the impact of it in the atmosphere of Pondicherry throughout the later period !

'Savitri' is not an ordinary woman. She is a subtle ray of divine consciousness. He who discovers this can feel this inner truth. When Manoj sat in his room and concentrated on composing the story of 'Laxmi's Adventure' , her soul used him as a medium for the great attempt. A person who is rich in general knowledge used his knowledge as mediums by a heavenly consciousness. One can no doubt feel the significance of the author's direct experience by studying Chandrasekhar Rath's book 'Mrutyu Arapariru Sanketa' (2003). If the Divine Consciousness can use the general consciousness for spiritual power, then supernatural powers like Manoj must be able to use that consciousness easily. The clear sign of it is this story. The purity of the soul of 'Savitri' is the best creation of Sri Aurobindo, which means that it is possible to find the same genius in the character of Laxmi. The author of this discussion can clearly feel that Pondicherry is not the name of a place, it is a land of consciousness. Manoj was reborn on that land. Laxmi's character is meaningless without portraying consciousness and discovering the underlying sentimentality in the story.

In the atmosphere of Pondicherry, Sri Aurobindo established a motherly appearance of 'Savitri', a symbol of great consciousness. Manoj had the magnetic power to grab her. Mysterious truth is manifested using Savitri as a medium of loving, compassionate, eternal mother. This does not mean that Laxmi was familiar with the life story of 'Savitri'. This consciousness exists but at a subtle level. Those who merely discover the similarity of content can never explain the subtle purpose and meaning of this matter.

The life stories of both Savitri and Laxmi are different. One can feel that Laxmi and Savitri are linked by a melody of auspicious music. Content must be secondary in this context. We can discover the same truth, which is established not in content, but in the inner light of the characters. It is a sincere blessing to the fate of the troubled human race.

Anyone who prays to the super-psychic power of Savitri, he must be blessed. In the story of 'Laxmi's Adventure' the priest also comes in contact with this consciousness and gains heavenly inspiration. Manoj is a soulful symbol of it. If analysed in this way, it is represented that the touch that was in Manoj's inner soul is an indication of the blessing of Sri maa. Laxmi is a transformative radiation of Savitri's inner soul. Because of this, the subtle philosophy 'Transformation of Consciousness' has been spontaneously revealed in the character of Laxmi.

Savitri is a great epic of love. Arguing with Yamaraj, Savitri is able to bring Satyavan's life back by engaging in deep love and devotion. By narrating the death of the priest in the 'Laxmi's Adventure' story, Manoj gives him the best reincarnation. It is meant for the perfection of the thoughts and consciousness of the human heart and life.

Gangadhar's Sita and Manoj's Laxmi

Why this comparison? The epic poem Tapaswini is composed by the poet Gangadhar Meher which is like Ramayana. It describes the story of Sita's rest life. The incidents in 'Laxmi's Adventure' are also known to everyone. As Laxmi's central thought grows deeper and deeper, the character of Sita in the poem 'Tapaswini' emerges and rises to the sky of consciousness. Sita is exiled by Lord Ramachandra because she is accused of being greedy and insulted by the people of Ayodhya. Sita neither expresses her anger towards Ramachandra nor blames the fellow people for her exile. Without blaming anyone, she silently sheds tears and says she is the cause of her sorrow and endures all the pain like a mother. She is a mother to all. Therefore, who will be equal to her in tolerance and infinite devotion, like mother earth!

Like Sita is exiled by the public for false accusations in 'Tapaswini', similarly in 'Laxmi's Adventure', Laxmi is condemned by the blind and ignorant people. The priest is only a representative of the crowd. As the priest and superstitious people utter derogatory words at Laxmi, any reader can feel the unbearable pain by placing himself in Laxmi's place for just a moment. Gangadhar writes about Sita- "When a palm tree is cut down with a sharp weapon and the juice is collected in the ground, just as the palm tree silently sheds its juice, Sati Sita also silently sheds her tears in the midst of all." Is the situation of Laxmi different from this? She enters the water of the pond and endures the harsh words of the priest as well as the people silently and calmly just like Sita.

What is the meaning of the tolerance of Sita or Laxmi? When we discover its true meaning, we can understand that these two goddesses have shown their infinite mercy to the people. Just as they forgive the cruel and blind masses in painful silence without complaining to anyone, it shows their immeasurable motherly love for the human race. From that point of view, there is a deep similarity between the two characters! Both of them have the same depth of affection.

Why this tolerance? Sita accepts the exile without any protest. Like Laxmi, she dies a terrible death. Is it meaningless? Great women with such divine power of consciousness are born in this world with a human body. In spite of all the falsehoods with their love and compassion, they melt the stony heart of a man. Its secret purpose is nothing else - to bring a change in human consciousness. For this, the people like the priest have changed. To lead from the path of evil to the path of truth, to lift man out of the womb, they endure the ignorance of all children like the loving and kind mother, with a generous heart.

There is no difference between the consciousness of Sita and that of Laxmi. In order to fulfil Ramachandra's vow, Sita accepts all the hardships. Laxmi endures all the tortures for her beloved God with infinite patience. She is just a little girl. The inner character of Laxmi cannot be revealed when the readers say that she is shocked by the behaviour of the priest and the people. She is shedding tears in her soul with fear. This great truth is reflected in her pain that her love, her attraction for God is as wide as the sky, and it is aimed at turning the consciousness of man towards the truth in a generous way. The mother endures all the ignorance of the child with her heavenly qualities. Sita is mother to all. Laxmi is also the best symbol of that motherhood. Both these characters are intended to free the afflicted earth from the darkness of ignorance and cruelty. That's why Sita of Tapaswini is so inspiring and alive that even after a hundred years, she is truly unique and admirable. Our beloved 'Mother Laxmi' is full of that same divine grace. Both of them have dedicated themselves to raise an answer to the human consciousness. Readers of 'Tapaswini' are enlightened in the experience of attaining rebirth; Readers of Manoj's 'Laxmi's Adventure' are also inspired to search for the ultimate truth after reading the story.

Sita and Laxmi, both sacrifice themselves in human consciousness. It will be considered a great blessing, no doubt. Both of the stories aim to reach at the innermost being and obtain the shining point of truth. Therefore, the readers have to remember both the characters.

Two feverish characters: a divine woman and a regretted child

Laxmi is not just a little girl. She is an incarnation of Goddess. The writer Manoj Das can discover the love of motherhood in every little girl. From that point of view, Laxmi is a little mother. But that is not the whole of her identity. Divine mother Sri maa appeared as the saviour of the priest in Manoj's writings.

We know very well both of the feverish characters; one is Laxmi and another is the priest. Both the characters died of fever. One is sick to change a human being's heart and another to hear the voice of a soul. Until the mystery of these two characters is revealed to us, we cannot imagine their importance. Human beings are filled with envy, arrogance and pride. It is purified by the devotion of life. We have no way to know about the birth and reincarnation of the Priest. But the way through which the priest changes at a special moment is determined by God. It is very important to make possible the extraordinary connection that the priest has with Laxmi. When Laxmi suffers from fever and departs from this earth, she leaves behind a divine vibration that pierce the heart of the Priest like an arrow. Amidst the meaningless noise of the crowd, the truth of God's existence felt invisibly. It's not possible for the priest to outline such a great truth. It is not his mind, but his innermost soul that sensed the truth. Therefore, in a single moment, the incident that happened to the priest made everyone speechless. "This sinner should be born without a tongue" - This heartfelt prayer comes from the innermost heart of the priest like tears. When a person has pride and suddenly the light of the divinity passes within him at that time a prayer can be made by him. That is what happened to the priest. What else could it be but the love of a divine mother? When Laxmi departs from this earth, a ray of bliss comes to the environment from which she emerges to the subtle world. Laxmi is a mother. She cannot get angry at the priest who treats her cruelly. She knows that her child has pride. Therefore, the final goal is to create a glimpse of blessings, not curse. We do not have the strength to see the sweetness of love in her last breath. It is a benevolent vibration of the invisible soul. That benevolent, auspicious, generous and loving vibration has always entered the soul of the priest. If the spirit of the priest had not received it, he might have returned in despair. Somewhere there is a soft soul hidden in the priest despite the outward harshness. Therefore, it is not too late for the priest to understand his own mistakes and arrogance. It is a palm tree bloomed in a moment under the sun, just as a lotus bloomed by the kiss of the moon. This feeling is extraordinary. It is supernatural. It is not the desire to be painful. It is the desire to be exalted. Can a harsh man be reawakened by a sweet cold touch? He who is filled with heat in his body, he can again feel the flood of fire in his heart. That is what happened in the priest's life. The divine fountain of eternal light has flowed in a momentary experience. There is no need to express more words. No one needs to explain anything. The lamp of his sincere love is burning like a pure candle in his heart.

The music of the prayer creates a unique emotion. It is a rare experience of emotional devotion. Only a lucky man can benefit from such glory. Only the critics can describe whether the last time of the Priest would have been satisfying or alive with the deepest compassion. Anybody's character cannot be judged just by the external appearance or from the spoken words. Without the ability and power to enter the inner soul, it would never have been imagined.

Laxmi looks very scared, depressed and pale. But only Laxmi's devotees are able to feel the manifestation of the divine mother in her. She is not an immature girl. She is a mother. The dry sleeping heart of the priest was moistened by her flow. Both of the characters are not as they appear. Every reader who can penetrate into her own soul can benefit from the affectionate opinion with which Manoj expresses the subtlest truths.

Just as Laxmi died of fever, the priest also departed from this world out of fever. Both of them are feverish. One is the Goddess mother and the another is her beloved child. Laxmi is playing the role of loving mother. The Priest has a soft-hearted soul devoted to her like a child. Therefore, the great writer Manoj Das has blessed the reader by depicting the death scenes of two characters with the same illness. In the rare moment when this story was composed, Manoj's thinking must be captured by a divine power. In the poem 'Tapaswini', the poet Gangadhar Meher praises maa Saraswati. According to his words, Manoj praises Sri maa to be an enlightened being. Sri maa descends from Manoj's holy faith. It will open our vision.

Conversation of Laxmi and God

The focus of this discussion is on the character Laxmi and on God described in 'Laxmi's Adventure' story by Manoj Das. In this story, the writer paints a realistic or emotional picture of a child who can communicate with God in a determined mind. Laxmi would never have come to the temple if God had not invited her in her dream to play. Game is nothing more; that is the connection of minds, to be absorbed, to be immersed in love with God. This is the best game in the world. In this game there is great pleasure. It is only in this game a man gets supernatural happiness. We cannot imagine the form in which God would have called Laxmi. That loving form is inside Laxmi. She alone can describe that form. The beautiful image of God in this story is not his outward appearance, it is his inner appearance, it is his emotional appearance. In the night, God complains to Laxmi that she is not playing with him. After hearing that from God, Laxmi always tried to enter the temple. But she cannot enter due to her fear for the priest. When the priest is sleepy at noon time, she enters the temple and meets God. According to Manoj Das "She speaks after observing the idol and his attire for two minutes." These two minutes of silence fill with a sweet passion that only God knows. Then Laxmi communicates with God in an easy and simple way like the conversation with a friend. She says to God that he should not eat all the bananas he has because his health will deteriorate if he eats all the bananas. After that, she asks God whether all forget mathematics like she forgets. But again, she said, 'No, you will not suddenly give a blessing to me. Maybe there is some good in mathematics. I am not mature enough to understand that.' This is expressed through the prayer that 'not my will but your will be done'. This prayer is the best prayer.

The way people sing songs on the microphone does not sanctify the whole environment but pollutes it. Prayer is never made with a roar. Then Laxmi made a request to God that devotion should be slowly instilled in everyone. She knows that great devotees like Dhruva Prahalad were not using a microphone to sing the songs of God. She can also feel at every moment that God can hear her even though she speaks quietly. Laxmi's feverish father closes his ears while the song is being played on these instruments. It means the roar of prayers is making someone else suffer. If society could realise the importance of this slow prayer, it is possible to imagine how much noise would be reduced. When Laxmi is asking her father for a frock, the angry man from whom he borrowed the money takes all the money from him. Laxmi says to mother that she will feel happy if she makes the frock out of her saree. People lie despite their unwillingness in life. When Laxmi's father is feverish, her mother informs the money lender that her father is not at home. Laxmi knows that her mother has lied. But when mother said to Laxmi in her tearful eyes, 'you will become a good human being. You will not lie even if you are in trouble.' Then Laxmi realised that even if her mother had lied, she cannot be a liar.

Laxmi's conversation with God in her dreams is more satisfying than the conversation she had in the daytime.

She is praying to God to appear again in her dreams. She also expresses her wish that if the priest falls asleep in such a quiet daylight, she must be able to reach God. What was the feeling of Laxmi when she came out from the temple? In Manoj's words, 'There is a bright light outside. She is confused for a while whether it is a day or night.'

After that, the compassionate chapter which is composed in the story, creates a painful moment for the readers. Why did Laxmi close her eyes in a few days? That's why there's unbearable sunlight in the outer atmosphere. It is strictly prohibited to exchange thoughts here. To connect hearts is forbidden here. It is a crime to associate with God. That's why she closes her eyes. Because she dreams of such a night, in which the real beauty of life lies. Laxmi appears as soulless to our eyes, but she closes her eyes to get the endless love of God forever. Night, not day, is needed for those who in a pure heart aspires to unite with God. For them, not the sun, but the moon is the only way.

There is no obstacle in the story to hear all the prayers of Laxmi. But what is Laxmi's feeling? Is she alone to talk to God? Not like this, God is also talking with Laxmi. An ordinary reader or writer does not have the power to hear those words. Even the writer Manoj becomes silent to form those words because God never speaks word after word like a human being. A flood of thoughts flow out of him incessantly. That unimaginable, inexpressible, determined soul knows the words of God for him. God gives appropriate answers to all her questions. Laxmi enters into God's heart in the silent temple without knowing the time of day or night. It's not possible to write the way through which God enters the soul of Laxmi in that silence.

The omnipresent God enters in Laxmi's body and

takes her to him. God knows very well that it is impossible for Laxmi to survive in this cruel harsh earth. That is why God has taken her to the emotional world where her two sweetest eyes can be exalted. Laxmi, who is soulless and silent for this mortal world, has become a soul of love in that emotional world. Therefore, what God said to Laxmi, Laxmi must have heard correctly. Even the writer Manoj Das heard that through his inner ear. How much we readers can hear is a question. The words of God, we can hear it in the deserted surroundings, in the stillness of the night and in the midst of pitch darkness. We can interact with God in the cool environment, between the sweet light of the stars. 'Laxmi's Adventure' is a message for all, that we can feel God only when we are close to a rare environment. In this intense sunlight and the atmosphere of intense human arrogance, we cannot create a suitable place to exchange human thoughts. This eternal call of God is expressed through Manoj's writings in a touching way, because Manoj has transformed his bosom into a suitable field of union between Laxmi and God. The day when this emotional relationship, emotional connection and wisdom in the world of Laxmi and God will disturb us, on that day we can also unite with Laxmi and God, as the priest is able to be compassionate at last.

Manoj Das's 'Aranyaka' and 'Laxmi's Adventure': A Comparative study

These two stories, considered to be Manoj Das's best-known works. The purpose of this study is to show how the consciousness of a writer in the early stages of his writing changes remarkably later on.

'Aranyaka' was written between 1956 and 1959 and compiled in the collection 'Aranyaka' in 1964. If we shed light on the contents of this story, the characters that emerge before us are Mr. Mitty, Mrs. Mitty, Mr. Chakodi, Raja Saheb and the driver Shymalendu. All of them have gone by a jeep on a dirt road to an abandoned bungalow, which is deep in the jungle. Their aim is to gain an exciting experience of life in the jungle. Through these characters, the author has opened the eyes of the readers to see the inside of them. They had guns in their hands. Mrs. Mitty instructs Shyamalendu, the driver, to kill a deer. But Shyamlendu could not do that because he said - "I cannot kill it. It's a pregnant hind." This shows that Shamalendu had a sensitive soul. If there is humanity among these people, it is only in Shyamalendu. Raja Saheb curses him for his stupidity. They have again gone hunting in the afternoon after a light lunch. But Shyamal is different. Raja Sahib is roaring at him as he politely refuses to go with them. It is noteworthy that Shyamal does not go with them. Mrs. Mitty also is not going with them. The reason is psychological. She wants to fulfil her physical desire with Shyamalendu. Shyamal behaves like a good boy with her, it fills Mrs. Mitty's mind with deep pain. How could a character like Mrs. Mitty remain silent without revenging that insult? When others come back to the bungalow, she brings a great complaint against Shyamal that he had misbehaved with her in the absence of others. All of them give physical injuries to Shyamal. In Mrs. Mitty's maddened laugh, Shyamal remains unconscious. These mad people bring a pig from their hunt. It is in a small room. They drag Shyamal into that room, close the door and window. They prepare a fire pit at the back of the bungalow. All these cruel characters sit there and drink. They drag the pig from the room and throw it into the fire. They cut the meat from it, sing songs and dance while eating it.

The next morning, they cannot remember whether they have eaten the pig or shyamala. It is clear in the story that they committed the crime in intoxication.

It is true that Manoj earned fame by composing such a thematic story. But can we rank it among his greatest achievements? Many critics have not only interpreted and praised the story, but also included it in the curriculum for students. Manoj Das's reputation as a fictionist is remarkable in all his classic works, and it is discussed from that point of view. The critics do not consider the thought and consciousness of Manoj Das while analysing this work. Manoj symbolises the essence of an evolutionary consciousness. He was once hopelessly close in human relations. This story is composed during that time. Therefore, even if the idea expressed in it regarding man is true, but it is not his final decision or idea.

In this context, 'Laxmi's Adventure' has captured everyone's heart as Manoj's best story. At the time of writing this story he had already got the vision of Sri Aurobindo and Sri maa. He is deeply aware that without a change in consciousness, it would not be possible for the human to rise to a higher level. Inspiring by Sri Aurobindo, Manoj touched the threshold from which man could utter the deep voice of hope and spirituality. While enveloped in such a great thought, he wrote the story 'Laxmi's Adventure'. The exchange of thoughts with the little girl Laxmi and God is really very heart touching. God resides in the simple and uncomplicated heart of a child. Manoj narrates this extraordinary story of Laxmi, and presents a character who is very human. The story of how the priest accuses Laxmi of being a thief over a trivial matter, how Laxmi jumps into the pond in fear, how the crowd does not understand Laxmi's heart, have shaken the hearts of the readers for decades. Everyone knows Laxmi's departure after severe fever from this world just three days later. When on Sunday evening the crowd gathered at the weekly epic reading, receiving evidence of God's presence the priest felt that God left the throne. Only his lightless, senseless form fell asleep. The blind people never see this sight. It is a rare sight that the mercy of God can be felt by them who can feel God. The priest may have received the grace of the previous birth. That is why he can see the clear and hidden form of truth. And at that moment, he becomes feverish. He comes to realise that he is responsible for Laxmi's death. Tears of regret break his heart. That's why he prays to God "Lord! In the next birth, this sin man must be born tongueless". This kind of prayer from a heart presents an enlightened aspect of human character that is truly close to divine consciousness.

No such voice of regret has been heard in the story 'Aranyaka'. There was no repent in their minds for the cruel behaviour they had shown in the drunken state of the night. Manoj Das has written both of the stories, 'Aranyaka' and 'Laxmi's Adventure'. The mood at the time of the composition of 'Aranyaka' and the composition of 'Laxmi's Adventure' are not the same. There is a great difference between the two. In one story, the ugly side of human beings' life has been exposed, while in another story, the flame of humanity is being composed which can illuminate all the dark areas in the interior with a soft light. The change in Manoj's perception of human relations is the main idea behind the composition of 'Laxmi's Adventure' story. Manoj has admitted this in multiple interviews. No matter how bad a person is, one can easily imagine the portrayal of the characters who feel that sweet spark of the soul.

In terms of fiction, 'Aranyaka' is a different creation. But in terms of art of life, 'Laxmi's Adventure' is his best creation. Sri maa has presented the essence of fiction in a positive mood. She says that by composing such a beautiful story, one can illuminate the human spirit. There is a detailed description of Sri maa, which can be found in the book 'Chirantani'. They alone can compose a beautiful story, who worship the deity in their inner souls. From that point of view, if we think and compare, then we can say the composer of 'Laxmi's Adventure' is more conscious than the composer of 'Aranyaka' in a touching way.

The sequence of consciousness in a writer continues who possesses evolutionary consciousness. Manoj is a sculptor of that level, who keeps himself exposed to the divine direction. That's why in his stories, human life is depicted in a more artistic way due to a significant change in his outlook in the later period. True art is that which glorifies the human spirit. Art which is created by basing on words and style does not have the sense of soul. When the author's style makes the reader accessible, the art becomes more relevant.

Oscar Wilde, the forerunner of the Art for art's sake movement whose stories also contain great messages for the well-being of human life which powerfully reveal the essence of art. In terms of all this, Manoj's fiction 'Tamosoma Jyotirgamaya' is covered with the sanctity of the verse. The story of 'Aranyaka' also provides an indirect motivation to free from passive behaviour. But 'Laxmi's Adventure' directly brings the reader's soul closer to divine consciousness.

Two rays of divine light: Rebati and Laxmi

Why do we Compare between these two characters, Revati and Laxmi ? No, comparison cannot be said. This is just a feeling of the same nature in both of the characters.

Such a thought appealed to the brain of the writer of this story, that is why Manoj Das is a great successor in Fakir Mohan's literary traditions. He himself admits that Fakir Mohan's influence was on him since childhood and adolescence. Fakir Mohan has portrayed Rebati's sad and bereaved life, it impressed the readers even after hundred years. The readers' hearts revolt against someone after thinking of how Rebati's life has sunk under so much grief. But who is the protagonist of this story - on which the readers will get angry. The story of 'Rebati' is an illustration of how human life can be tragic even without the antagonist. How has the orthodox race endured this pain for hundreds of years? Is it the pain and hardship to bear? Even if they protest, this nation has been making an experience since years that all their efforts will become meaningless.

In this context, when Manoj's 'Laxmi' character comes to our mind, the soul trembles. As Fakir Mohan describes it, when Rebati ascends to heaven, the divine mother has reached to take her innocent soul towards her. That divine ray combined with the divine mother and again brings

Laxmi to the earth. The soul born from the mother, comes down to the bosom of the earth in a new form. Rebati is Laxmi and Laxmi is Rebati.

In the story 'Rebati', there may not be any negative character, but here human luck is the root cause of all these sufferings. Why did Manoj Das, the successor of Fakir Mohan, tolerate this decision? The creation of Laxmi's character is a brilliant counterpoint to Rebati's character.

Rebati is affected by Nature. The master priest and the heartless masses, by whom the little Laxmi is tortured are a bad sign of this cruel era. Fate, which pulls man's life, Makes the heart like mud; Can that fate really be eternal and ever holy? For this reason, Sri Aurobindo and Sri maa have deeply felt how this earth and human life are deeply harmed by fate. That is why they have the promise of enlightening this world covered in the darkness of ignorance. For this reason, in Manoj's writing, Rebati has appeared on this earth in the form of Laxmi. As Rebati is silent, here Laxmi is also silent at the cruel priest and at the treatment of the ignorant masses. Neither Rebati told anything nor Laxmi uttered a single word to the priest and heartless crowd.

Both of them are an expression of the spirit of silence, stillness and innocence. Does this silence never speak any language! The language of silence is more powerful than spoken words. Laxmi has given up her soul, in the same silence Rebati also died. We cannot even imagine how strong its influence can be. To endure the great result of fate means that the night of eternal darkness may end for mankind. Not only for herself, she has endured the sorrows and misfortunes of the entire human race for the arrival of the future. Just like Laxmi in the story of 'Laxmi's Adventure' is a radiant character of extraordinary endurance, Rebati too has endured all her sorrows for an extraordinary sunrise. That sunrise is nothing but the priest's transformation of the inner soul. This change is only an indication. A bright light of great consciousness against the darkness of ignorance. Both characters are not only meant to change the heart of man. It is a glimpse of light against the evils of the present ignorance of the earth.

There is no need to explain everything in a story. Even the writer himself does not need to understand everything. Sometimes the author knowingly provides the clues to understand. Fakir Mohan has not explained everything in Rebati's story. But he says everything through the character of Rebati. Similarly, through the character of Laxmi, without saying Manoj describes the luminous consciousness that controls the souls. These two characters have endured all sorrows, injuries and attacks of life for a better future. Fakir Mohan sheds his ceaseless tears to save her from the misery that holds her destiny. Laxmi's extraordinary tolerance is meant to change the ignorance that has taken root in the human heart and prevents it from manifesting its true form. To realise the level of consciousness that the creator Manoj has provided, we need inner introspection. Fakir Mohan is the emperor of spoken literature. Manoj is his best follower. Manoj had the power to carry the flame of Fakir Mohan's soul. That is why the character of 'Laxmi' has emerged from that burnt soul.

These two characters have suffered a lot due to their great age. But both are in the glory of eternal life. They became the future life of men in a meaningful silence which can only be discovered by the devotees. It is time for us to pray earnestly by paying our devotional prayers to these two timeless characters.

Manoj Das's 'Laxmi's Adventure' and Oscar Wilde's 'The Selfish Giant': A Comparative study

Manoj Das is a unique writer in Odisha who has gained fame at the national and international level. It is idealistic that this great writer, who felt attracted to Marxism in his student life, opened his heart to the philosophy of Sri Aurobindo later on. When he started composing stories, he strongly evoked the sorrow, misery and helplessness of men. He also evoked the harshness and brutality that is filled in the human psyche, he also strongly presented it as a real artist. That is why the fame of his stories like 'Aranyaka' has not faded till now. But 'Aranyaka' may be regarded as his best creation by those critics who are not aware of the later evolution of Manoj' ideal. Due to this lack of awareness, this story has been included many times in the curriculum for the college or university students. Manoj himself very honestly admits that his soul from the beginning was covered in pessimism and later in contact with the consciousness of Sri maa and Sri Aurobindo filled with optimism. In this regard, if we consider him, he is not only in the world of Odia fiction, but also in the field of world literature. He is the one who spreads the rays of great inspiration.

The actual readers have connected their souls with the

fictions of Oscar Wilde. Those who are serious readers of English literature know that Oscar Wilde is a novelist of the highest thinking, not writing stories for trivial entertainment. He also excelled in writing to answer humanity. Manoj Das himself is aware of Oscar Wilde, but to think that he composed the stories under his influence, would certainly not be justified. Oscar Wilde's soul was connected to the soul of the Lord Jesus Christ in his forgiving consciousness. The soul of Manoj Das touched by the blessings of Sri maa and was immersed in the divine light. So Sri maa became the source of inspiration for both of the writers. We can say that a great being is an example of endless compassion. The world famous novelist Oscar Wilde was immersed in literature in Dublin, Ireland in the late nineteenth century. It is not the reason to represent the significance of Manoj's story based on that in modern times. Although the time, place and language are different, the form of consciousness between both of them is very perceptible.

Oscar Wilde has written many stories. The story named 'The Selfish Giant' is very popular among the readers. Similarly, Manoj is the composer of influential stories, only his readers know it better. His 'Laxmi's Adventure' story gained popularity in Odisha and outside Odisha. It is not only popular within Odia language or Odisha, but it glorifies and illuminates the dark soul of men.

What happened in the 'Laxmi's Adventure' story? Laxmi is a little girl. She dreams and Communicates with God. In the afternoon, when the environment is empty, she rushes to the temple with great emotion in her heart. Passing the priest, who is sleepy, she reaches God. At that time of solitude, she describes her thoughts one by one to God. She cannot escape from the angry eyes of the priest while leaving the temple after taking two bananas from God. She runs and enters into the pond. The priest accuses her as a banana thief and utters harsh words to her. Laxmi's father comes and rescues her from the pond. Then Laxmi closes her eyes out of fever. When people give Haribol after getting the proof of God's existence, the priest, who accuses her of theft, realises at that moment that God has left the throne. His inner eyes open. He sees the deity has left the throne. Only his lightless, meaningless form lies. The story is not over. The priest himself suffers from fever. His heart is bleeding on the death of Laxmi. He prays to God, "May this sinful soul born tongueless in the next birth." This surprising ending of the story leaves the reader's soul deeply tempted. The readers wonder for the priest who was so cruel, now his soul is deep in tears. Similarly, the wall of pride within the reader also breaks down.

Those who are great writers, they never get satisfaction by portraying the ugly form in man. On the contrary, they get that ultimate satisfaction by drawing the softness of the human soul. Just as Manoj Das is a divine grace in Odia and Indian literature, so in world literature, the English writer Oscar Wilde has effectively exposed the human consciousness. Oscar Wilde's story 'The Selfish Giant' is remarkable. Wilde has introduced a character who is like the character of the priest. In the story, the character of this selfish man is like a monster, and he has a beautiful garden. The children play in the garden. It is surrounded by trees, flowers, green grass, butterflies and birds. But this selfish man, the owner of the garden, very cruelly forbade the children to enter. What happened next that shakes human consciousness. What happened? The Children are not able to enter after the ban. The leaves wither and fall due to it. No more beautiful and fragrant flowers bloom on the trees. The spring no longer visits that garden. One day, that selfish giant suddenly hears the melody of sweet music and smells the sweet fragrance floating in the breeze from the petals of the flowers. Leaving the house, he sees the children are playing in the garden by jumping over the wall. After getting the touch of the children, the soil of the garden becomes fertile. The beauty of the flowers on the trees has made him lose his confidence. This one strange incident has shattered the cruelty within him instantly. His heart is overflowing with love. After playing with those children, he gets immense pleasure. Gradually, he became old and reached old age. He can't play with the children anymore. Sitting on a chair, he is watching their faces, bright looks and joyful play. In such a situation, he realises that flowers are beautiful, but these children are the most beautiful and fragrant flowers. This selfish man gains the heavenly happiness of living. Then he changes into a selfless affectionate and loving man. In that garden, he comes in direct contact with such a divine boy who is none other than the symbol of Jesus Christ. By the touch of this divine boy, his life changes and he becomes heavenward by gaining his mercy. In 'Laxmi's Adventure', who has revealed herself in this character of Laxmi? This Laxmi is none other than divine mother 'Sri maa'. To transform human cruelty into tenderness she embraces death through Manoj's writings. Whether Manoj Das is aware of this or not does not matter. It is up to them how to interpret divine spirits such as the divine mother or Lord Jesus Christ. In this case, Oscar Wilde or Manoj Das are excellent, through which the expression of divine consciousness can take place very heartily.

We don't know that Manoj composed 'Laxmi's Adventure' after getting inspiration from this story of

Oscar Wilde. It is also beyond our knowledge that which story inspired Oscar Wilde to write 'The Selfish Giant'. Both artists are connected to that divine source from which shines the clear rays of God's infinite mercy. The comparison in both the stories is presented because a great power has been working silently and uninterruptedly in order to transform this earth into a divine form. Children are the most beautiful expression of beauty and grace. The way God changes the cruel men is unimaginable. Such stories in world literature make the lotus bloom in the human soul.

Manoj Das, who has a pure soul inspired by Sri Aurobindo and Sri maa, resided in Pondicherry and brought the divine way of life to earth. Oscar Wilde may not have lived in a churchyard; but the consciousness in which he established his soul was not far from the divine world shown by Sri Aurobindo. In one story, the sweetness of Lord Jesus Christ's compassion, and in another story, divine mother Sri maa's sacrifice and divine compassion flowed. The role played by both writers in unifying the human soul, in connecting man with the voice of his inner soul, is a surprising example in the world of realistic literature. It is powerful in its ability to illuminate with rays of compassion. In this regard, both authors should be honoured and both stories should be treated in the glory of being timeless.

An expression of the desire of divine Mother: 'Laxmi's Adventure' and 'Nivedita ra Naishavisara'

Those who are the conscious readers of modern fiction or devoted readers of Manoj Das know not only about the content of 'Laxmi's Adventure' story but also about its artistic achievement and its success in revealing the essence of human life. Similarly, another great story writer of this period is Mahapatra Neelamani Sahu. By composing a long story titled 'Nivedita ra Neishavisara', he earnestly prays to reveal the essence of divine consciousness. Neelamani's 'Nivedita ra Neishavisara' does not get the same popularity as Manoj's story 'Laxmi's Adventure' does. So we have to keep in mind that both these writers were inspired by the philosophy of Sri Aurobindo. In the consciousness of both of them, the presence of Sri Aurobindo and Sri maa is absolutely true and real.

In the stories of famous English writer Oscar Wilde, the style of Jesus Christ's compassion is directly reflected. Similarly, in the collection of stories of Manoj Das and Mahapatra Neelamani Sahu, the light of Sri Aurobindo and Sri Maa's divine consciousness is reflected. Leo Tolstoy, a Russian writer, is particularly memorable in his field for providing the idea of God.

The essence of Sri Aurobindo's philosophy is the transformation of consciousness. A wild man or a monkey is considered as the ancestor of a man. Similarly, the divine form of God has inspired many prominent literary figures in India, as depicted by Sri Aurobindo. Manoj Das and Mahapatra Neelmani Sahu are important and creative writers among them. In 'Laxmi's Adventure' story, the picture of a little girl Laxmi, who exchanged her feelings with God in the temple during the lonely afternoon is vividly drawn. When she brings two bananas from the temple, the priest shows his cruel heart to her. The way the priest chases Laxmi and many people of the village run after her make her panic. She enters into a pond and hides there for a long time. Later, her father comes and rescues her from it and takes her away. The little girl dies suddenly. By this the priest realises that God has abandoned the temple and left only his idol lifeless. The priest accepts fever and suffers by blaming himself for Laxmi's death. That painful situation has suddenly given him a rare chance of regeneration. His tone with great repentance has surprised the readers. The priest curses himself and says - "May this sinner born without a tongue in the next birth." It may seem like a curse but it is not a curse but a sign of divine manifestation of divine mother in him. The life which left the idol in the temple has entered into this priest and transformed him instantly. Dasyu Ratnakara's appearance in the form of Valmiki, the violent Angulimala's disturbance for the love of Buddha are the examples. This transformation is not possible in a moment. This can only be possible by the Almighty's grace. Through Manoj's writing in the form of Laxmi, Sri maa herself appears as a living idol and she could have changed the heart of the cruel priest in just a moment. If such a change can be found at the time of death, it can never be regarded as a sign of death but a divine rebirth. In this regard, it is not possible for Manoj Das to have been aware of the writing. By basing on a single clear creative consciousness, God can manifest himself. So, Manoj Das is only a medium. His great desire for eternal life has created an eternal sound in his soul for the descent of this spirit. A reader who keeps the image of God's presence in his heart, can't forget the story 'Laxmi's Adventure'. In this regard, anyone can feel the discovery of motherly love in Manoj's great consciousness.

This is the time to discuss the story 'Nivedita ra Neishavisara' written by Mahapatra Neelamani Sahu. This story is not just an ordinary love story. Heroine Nivedita wrote a long letter in this story on Saturday, May 26, 1984, at 9:30 PM. In this letter, she has mentioned her mother-in-law, father-in-law, and her husband. It means that she is married. Even after marriage, the desire of her heart remains unfulfilled. Because she is not just a simple woman made of ordinary elements. Her personality is extraordinary. She is a brave woman. The determination she has adopted is the recognition of a unique great human being. Her decision is that she will leave home tonight to pursue her goal. What is her goal then? Her father is her most beloved person. Since her childhood, he has covered her consciousness as if it were a proof of her extraordinary personality. Nivedita is very beautiful. Her manners, behaviours, maturity of growth, and knowledge have impressed many men. But no one is able to enter her heart. What does a woman really want in her life? She herself got the answer that it is 'joy'. Where does this joy come from? She confirmed that it is obtained from love. But it is the misfortune of human beings that knowingly or unknowingly they run behind this love and when they are close to this true love, they cannot feel it. However, there is nothing but love which makes life easy. With the desire of that love, she reaches the male friends. The readers can feel that the common man is unable to satisfy the love desires of this extraordinary woman. She cherishes a great man who would be as wide as the sky. He must have covered Nivedita's entire heart and soul. That great man would be entering her soul through inhalation and coming out again through exhalation. More unimaginable idea is that the time between every inhalation and exhalation should be filled by the same hero.

She has left home to find a life partner with such a noble and generous consciousness, and hopes that she must meet the hero of her dreams. Such a desire will never be irreplaceable, if it is written in luck.

The image of Sri maa of Pondicherry emerges in front of the readers who are aware of her or when they read the whole story 'Nibedita ra Neishavisara' in one breath. Sri maa is an extraordinary mother who was born in France. She married twice. She was also blessed to be the mother of a child, but in her dream she saw a great man with extraordinary consciousness. That dream has been fulfilled, after her departure to India. The feelings Sri maa expresses when she meets Sri Aurobindo at Pondicherry is what Nivedita would have expressed if she could have met the hero of her dreams in the story.

The way in which Sri maa surrenders to Sri Aurobindo by accepting the final decision and giving up her worldly life we can say that it is a great union of two consciousnesses. Therefore, it will never be wrong to say that in this story Mahapatra Neelamani Sahu represents the great desire of the inner consciousness of Sri maa. The brilliant writer like Mahapatra Neelmani Sahu keeps himself oriented towards the divine light of Sri maa which manifests itself in the form of 'Nivedita' with extraordinary form.

Manoj Das has been dedicated to Sri maa in Sri Aurobindo monastery since 1963. Although Mahapatra Neelmani Sahu does not get the chance to stay in Sri Aurobindo's monastery, he gains the heart-warming heavenly touch of Sri maa's compassion by staying in Pondicherry. Therefore, these two writers dedicated their souls to the divine consciousness. So we can see the revelation of Sri maa's inner consciousness in both stories. Just as 'Laxmi's Adventure' provides the motivation for human transformation, similarly, 'Nivedita ra Neishavisara' provides a loving and compassionate consciousness. So these two stories are not ordinary for the reader's entertainment. It is not the goal of both the writers to create general joy or excitement. Both of them are associated with the dream of Sri Aurobindo and Sri maa for a divine life. As a result of that unique connection, the composition of two stories 'Laxmi's Adventure' and 'Nivedita ra Neishavisara' became possible. Two writers are like two great monks who have tried to take human beings to the deepest level of consciousness. By reading these two stories, no doubt the reader's heart will rise with an extraordinary light of love. Two stories should not be limited to Odisha only, but must be considered as two extraordinary creations of Indian literature and world literature.

Sri Aurobindo and Sri maa imagined a new world. The literary scholars who came close to them, realised the essence of Sri Aurobindo's philosophy and also realised the height of Sri maa's personality by which they are able to create such wonderful heroes and heroines. Manoj Das and Mohapatra Neelmani Sahu know how consciously they write Sri maa and Sri Aurobindo. But we cannot deny the fact that even in their ignorance, the radiance of Sri maa's personality can be reflected in their compositions. So in many respects we accept the divine inspiration that these two stories give us for our consciousness, through which the light of life of our readers can be revealed.

In the story 'Laxmi's Adventure', Laxmi enters the temple at the call of God in the afternoon. Normally she communicates with God. In the story 'Nivedita ra Neishavisara', Nivedita listens to the call of her soul in a silent night, starts her journey to her desired hero and leaves the world. In the language of the great Sri maa, who else can be that divine soul without God?

The difference is reflected in 'Laxmi's Adventure' while changing the heart of the priest. Nivedita is not praying for her imaginary husband to satisfy her lust. Because the writer has already admitted that her soul is not satisfied with the physical satisfaction. What will she do after her union with her hero ? Her soul must be disturbed by the feeling of heavenly love. Her role is not ending there. She remains with her lover to bring heavenly love into her. It may not be clear in the story. But this is her duty and for this she comes to this earth. Mahapatra Neelamani Sahu believes, those who are highly conscious, never feel satisfied after getting their love. They dream of covering the whole earth with love, and therefore get pain to spread heavenly love. That's why Nivedita mentions in her letter, "A little higher than us, the love jar full of nectar is tied to the branches of the tree and we all die without satisfying thirsts." ' (p. 143)

Therefore, can Nivedita make devotion for those who would die without love on this earth? In order to get such love, the heroes and heroines who can make this earth musical by the exchange of mutual love, for them there are tears from the eyes of kind men. That is why, at last of the story the writer is saying, "For these Supreme men and women who are eternally desirous for love, many auspicious beings from the bosom of space are constantly showering divine flowers." (p. 150)

Really, 'Laxmi's Adventure' and 'Nivedita ra Neishavisara' in our world of literature are like two divine flowers - from which the sunshine of human pain on this earth will be removed and divine love and joy will be established. This thought must be strengthened in us.

'The Letter of the Last Spring' and 'Laxmi's Adventure' : two divine daughters

Why the comparison between the two little goddess idols? The answer is that both the stories depict the characters of the two little girls, which inspires such a comparative analysis. All the readers have realised that these two stories are unforgettable. The name of the little girl who appears in 'The Letter of the last spring' is Reena. What is the real significance of Reena? That is the expression of motherly love that is hidden in her heart. The writer describes in the story that Reena is waiting on the road which is on the opposite side in front of her house. She is waiting for the postmaster to receive a letter from his mother. But the letter never reaches her. There is not an end to her waiting. She keeps a letter from her mother like a precious gem. Her mother was admitted to the hospital due to illness and wrote a letter to her daughter. The love she has expressed for Reena, after reminding that love the whole body feels excited. The sympathetic words of hope and assurance that the mother is writing for the girl have been very heart-warming for the readers since decades.

Reena is keeping her mother's letter very carefully. The emotion of the gentleman or the writer who looks to the road in front of her house is more surprising. She thinks that just as she is anxious to get her mother's letter, the writer is also waiting for his mother's letter. Reena doesn't know that her mother is no more in this world. For this she is not getting any letter from her. She feels the same pain the writer must be getting like her because he is also waiting for a letter from his mother. How great is the maternal consciousness which is revealed in the little girl Reena? She feels that if the gentleman is in pain like her, the words written in her mother's letter may bring peace and love to his troubled heart. That's why when Reena sends her mother's letter to the writer, the writer gets emotional and says in a painful tone, 'Reena, my little mother.'

Why does Laxmi come to mind after reading this story? Manoj Das says that he sees the glory of motherhood in every little girl. But in the story of 'Laxmi's Adventure', is Laxmi writing any letter? No, not at all. So why this discussion today? This discussion means for the reason that the way Laxmi enters the temple, chased away by the priest, enters into the pond and after being rescued by her father, just two or three days later the way she dies is very heart touching like Reena's letter. This is an 'unwritten letter' of Laxmi. A unique earthquake has been created in the heart of the priest after reading the letter. Just as the writer in 'The Letter of the Last Spring' says that Reena is his mother, similarly, in the story of 'Laxmi's Adventure' the priest can see the image of Laxmi within himself. He could say after such an insight came to him, 'This sinner may be born without a tongue.' It is impossible for such a language without the feel of the divine mother. The priest is feeling remorse – it is the immense compassion of Mother Laxmi. After she herself left, she took back her cruel son after breaking the stone heart.

Letters are not just written on paper. The breeze, the sunlight and the floating clouds pass the language of the heart. It is surprising that such a language, to a specific person, can be delivered at a faster speed than a missile. Reena and Laxmi - both are the manifestations of heavenly affections. Reena's emotional words are expressed. The thoughts of Laxmi's heart are covered in an expressive style of love. That is why he, who is little insightful, can feel how life changes. That is why, both Reena and Laxmi are such glorious symbolic expressions of the divine that make the world of literature pure and free like the sacred stream of Ganga. It cannot be assumed that Manoj thought these deeply. A timeless story that has been composed from the warm and excited heart. A reader's soul can feel wonderful after reading the rare similarities between these two stories.

'Groom for Sita' and 'Laxmi's Adventure '

'Groom for Sita' is a heart touching story in Manoj Das's compilation of stories. In this story, Manoj describes the marriage of contractor Lalbabu with Jyosthna, the eldest daughter of Basanti. The next character is Sita. Professor Devbabu's daughter Sita expresses her heart-felt anger because her parents did not wake her at the time of the marriage ceremony. She complains that no one woke her up at the marriage of Basanti. Her tender heart and two anxious eyes were very eager to see the marriage. That's why she proposes to marry her father. The father informed that he had already married her mother. After hearing this, Sita is getting angry. She thinks that her parents are so Selfish that they married without her presence. However, father tried to explain that she was not born then. But she is not ready to accept that she was not there during their marriage. She thinks she will marry when her father is asleep. Dev Babu said this is correct because if she will marry, she is able to see the marriage. And there is no need to go to anyone's house. A new problem arose after this. Where is the groom? She finds some are married, and some others are cruel to whom she doesn't like. She is upset after hearing from her father that she needs a lot of money for marriage. In between, Sita has discovered another truth that after marriage Basanti is often crying. Basanti's father has given a lot of money to her in-laws house, but her engineer husband often gets angry with her, attacks her with a liquor bottle and breaks her nose. Her life is a mystery. When the old grandfather came to her, she was asking to get a groom. The grandfather says - "From where I will bring a groom for my Sita Without Ramachandra himself." After hearing this one line from the grandfather, her face fills with immense joy. How can she get Ramachandra? The old man tells her that if Sita calls Ramachandra from her heart, he will surely come. Then she smiles. She tells her grandfather that she will call him tonight. She requests her grandfather not to tell about this to her parents. Everyone is asleep in their routine life. In the morning, when Sita wakes up from her sleep, Devbabu surprises after seeing her face. Manoj writes that Sita's face is full of seriousness. But she doesn't say much, only smiles, that smile fills with compassion. She is in a different world, it's not possible for her parents to reveal the secret. Her parents failed to bring her to the previous state. They come to know that Sita married Ramachandra, with the presence of heavenly musical instruments and angelic garlands. It is not just a dream for Sita. It is more true and real to her than the reality of the visible world. The seriousness on Sita's face is the same. Meanwhile, they hear about Basanti's suicide. After hearing this, Sita is going to ask her spirit - which is the dream? Basanti's marriage or my marriage?

Many years passed since the writer separated from Devbabu. Now Sita is eligible for marriage. Her father is in search of a good groom. But Sita rejects that proposal. She became silent and silent forever after a short illness.

After explaining the story 'Groom for Sita', is it necessary to reveal the mystery of the story 'Laxmi's Adventure'? Such goddesses are born on this earth who are sent by God and return to him at the end. In the story 'Laxmi's Adventure', there is no description of Laxmi's marriage. That is unnecessary too. Sita Surrenders to Ramachandra is very deep and mysterious like the way Laxmi converses with God. Sita is dedicated to Ramachandra and Laxmi is dedicated to God. Such deities can never establish the emotional relations with human beings who live in the worldly life. They eventually return to that subtle world from which they descended. How can common men have the ability to marry such goddesses? Sometimes they take the name of 'Sita', sometimes the name of 'Laxmi', sometimes the name of 'Radha' and sometimes they come down with the name of 'Mira' in order to light a divine candle in the society and in the human mind. Their minor illness is not really minor. It is like the close touch and intimate embrace of the warm hands of their beloved. If we think that Laxmi is ill due to the priest's cruel treatment, then it may not be true at all. The priest is only the source. Laxmi's landing for him is another deep and serious matter for characterisation. Had it not been the virtues of the priest, he would never have had the good fortune to come in contact with Laxmi. The great message Laxmi gives to the entire society will shine forever after the priest's change of heart. In the story of 'Groom for Sita', there is no such change of character; but the appearance of Sita's dream-vision to the world is a meaningful reality. The way that she is united to Ramachandra in her dream is eternally true and real than the marriage of Basanti. Suicide is the option in unreal and reckless life. And a little bit of sickness happens for a character like Sita in the midst of mystical reality, faith and hope. Suicide corrupts the aim of a person. Sita's slight illness makes the character reach the target. This is the unreal - where disrespect and hatred and arrogance are spread. And on the contrary that is the reality where one gets the extraordinary fortune to be absorbed in devotion. It is not easy to uncover the secret hidden in Mira's love for Sri Krishna's idol. Similarly, discovering Sita's arrival to this earth is also a difficult matter. Only those who have intimate attachment to the world are inspired to enter in this matter. It is impossible for those who are misguided in the vile worldliness to understand its symbol.

The soul of the character Sita in 'Groom for Sita' story is also made of the same element as the soul of Laxmi. Both of them have come to this earth from a subtle place. Both are reunited with their ever-desired God, and both return to their beloved God after suffering from the same illness. The eternal message of the story 'Groom for Sita' is not to take external reality as the absolute truth and keep the heart open to the beauty of the subtle world. The message in the story of 'Laxmi's Adventure' is to transform the human heart that we are born with into a divine one. A writer who is the composer of a story like 'Groom for Sita' is only capable of creating stories like 'Laxmi's Adventure'. Sita in Manoj's heart is similar to Sita in his words and Stories. The same Sita appears again with the name Laxmi in the story of 'Laxmi's Adventure'. Only two different names of the same soul in the same universe. They are the two names of divine thought. It is quite difficult to describe how these two shake the hearts of the readers. It is quite obvious to remind Sita after reading the character of Laxmi. Both of them have the same creation. Reminding both Sita and Laxmi together is capable of touching the reader's heart. This is our silent thought.

'Sarvabhuteshu' and 'Laxmi's Adventure'

One can feel the inner truth expressed differently in Manoj Das's various stories after reading the same truth in 'Laxmi's Adventure' story. Another important story is 'Sarvabhuteshu' in the compilation named 'The Dusky Horizon and other stories'. A portrait of a baby boy with three other characters of this story appeals to the soul. In the story, the land owner has given instructions to Naib to cure his animal hunger. Naib is helpless and he has invited a girl against his own will. Her name is Lalitha. She is dumb. Naib is disturbed by the silence that is flashing on Lalitha's face in the stormy rain. But he is helpless. Sometimes God could sense the helplessness of such a situation at the right time. The unsatisfied Character – The ardent landlord has not been able to satisfy his desire; because just at that time his motherless son reached the court. The great truth which neither Naib nor the landlord could perceive, has arisen in the soul of the infant son. He has painted the portrait of Lalita's similar look throughout the night. What a strange encounter! This little boy is like an angel. The baby boy has expressed that idea through his drawing, which was neither in the mind of the landlord nor in the mind of Naib.

The night passed. The drawing is not complete. At this time Naib reached there. He comes to know through his intuition that the purpose for which he brought Lalita to the landlord, that purpose has not been fulfilled. He finds such a light in Lalitha, as a result of which he is on the ground and utters "mother! Kill me or save me - whatever you want." Unknowingly, his two hands are also joined with palms for the sake of Lalitha.

What do we see in this story? Naib and the Landlord here represent the cruel Priest. Lalitha is none other than the Laxmi character. What is hidden in the way in which the priest blames himself for Laxmi's death and curses himself. It is the ultimate secret of experiencing Laxmi's divine motherhood. Not only does the priest see the form of God's idol inside the temple, but he can see in his divine eyes that Laxmi is not just an ordinary girl. She is a great part of Divine Mother. There is no difference between the brutality of the landlord to satisfy his desire and the harsh language of the priest towards the little girl Laxmi. The cruelty in human beings is equal to the wildness in them. In the story of 'Sarvabhuteshu', the motherless son of the landlord shows the extraordinary light to Naib and landlord. The priest in 'Laxmi's Adventure' story tells harsh words to Laxmi. The cruelty and harshness in men is the same just like the passive desire in them. In the story of 'Sarvabhuteshu', the motherless son of the landlord sees the extraordinary light in the eyes of Lalita in the mirror of his simple heart that the Naib or the landlord could not see. If he had not arrived that night and if he had not been absorbed in the joy of painting Lalitha, Naib or the landlord would not have the opportunity to feel Lalitha's divine motherhood. Like the death of Mahishasura by Durgashakti, Naib surrenders near the feet of Lalita. The truth which is not arising in the conscious mind of the landlord has bewildered him for a moment. On the one hand, the sacred image of the baby boy and on the other hand Naib's character who can feel the Goddess of beauty and compels the landlord to join hands with a devoted heart.

Manoj Das's story does not end with the heavenly light that shines in a little girl. The matriarchy that exists within the female has unconsciously found shelter in the portrayal of the characters like Lalita. These two characters 'Laxmi' and 'Lalita' are one and the same symbolic image of one power. The priest, Naib and the landlord are symbols of the cruel nature of men. In 'Laxmi's Adventure' story, the priest dies and remains safe in the protective circle of the divine mother. Similarly, Naib and the Landlord are also enlightened by Lalita in the 'Sarvabhuteshu' story. They surrendered. It is the sin in both of them - the impurity of the dark mind, which is faded away by the forgiveness of Lalita. The deep inspiration that inspired Manoj's heart to draw such a character is truly relevant in the present day. Both these stories are a powerful counterpoint to the society's neglected girl children and the harsh treatment towards them. There is no question of Manoj writing such stories, imbued with an advertising attitude. It is the glorious manifestation of the inner light of his soul. If the reader of such a story has the humble humanity that remains hidden within, then he must be able to listen to the inner voice of such a supreme being. The uniqueness of Manoj's writing spirit can be felt by noting both these stories express the same great truth differently.

Raibabu in 'Teeth' and the priest in 'Laxmi's Adventure'

There is a deep meaning of the story *Teeth* in the compilation named as 'The Dusky Horizon and other stories'. The character Roy babu, who is very rough and harsh, is brought before the readers with a special purpose. The writer himself is embarrassed and frightened by the harshness of this character. But later he is shocked to see the transformation in him. He has two sons, Babu and Sabu. After their marriage, the harsh behaviour of the in-laws-daughters has crushed his pride. He is in old age. The character, who had shown harsh behaviour towards the children throughout his life, becomes affectionate towards them in the last stage of his life. This is his true nature. Manoj notices such a change in characters and gives the best expression to the beauty of his personality in just one line. The most memorable line is "His false teeth were scattered on the table, the smile of his toothless mouth looking delightful".

Manoj loves the pure smile and sanctity of his mouth, not artificial teeth. This artificial inner form is revealed when man is able to give up unnecessary pride and arrogance. The treatment he received from his sons-in-law made him completely free from all artificiality.

How can the character of the priest be compared with the Roy babu of this story? The themes of these two stories are different, the characters are also different, but the same truth can be found in both of the stories. The rudeness of the priest in 'Laxmi's Adventure' is not at all different from the rudeness of Roy Babu. Roy Babu changes due to the circumstances and the priest is tormented by guilt and thinks to experience rebirth. The readers know very well about the painful condition of the priest. It is not easy to explain the way the priest understood the futility of his rude behaviour. He prays to get punishment for the cruel behaviour he has shown towards Laxmi. So at the end of this story, the smile on the face of the priest is beyond imagination. So how is it possible to compare it with Roy Babu's story 'Teeth'? In this way, if one tries to see these two characters together, he can find that one's face shows a heavenly light, while the another's face burns with remorse.

When a character cries after realising his mistake, and when another character's lips are filled with a holy and prideless smile because of the realisation of that mistake - both of these scenes represent the same truth. It is our hope that after such a question no one would realise the need to explain the answer. The expression that emerges on a repented face, the readers can find the same expression reflected in a toothless mouth. The appearance of the two faces is different. But the thoughts and feelings are exactly the same. Manoj describes the smile of a toothless mouth as very pleasant. Does the beauty on the priest's mouth reflect like that? There is no restriction on making the answer available to the poor readers. Because the same inner beauty can be found on a happy face and on a painful face. It is needless to say that the two characters of these two stories are not different at all. The beauty seekers only know when the feelings of a realised heart reflects on eyes and faces, it looks very attractive. The priest is shaking with fever. But his soul fills with an extraordinary joy. Who else can express it except him ?

The similarity between the two characters in these two stories is revealing the same absolute truth. Roy babu and the priest have different personalities; but the condition of the dark mind in both are the same. This unique similarity of these characters is the real reflection of our life. It is important to depict the heart of a man, not his ambitions. Manoj Das has drawn the great image to convey that a man can achieve his goal no matter what the path is, if the goal is fixed in his mind. In this regard, it is a hope that everyone can hear the music that is played in both of these two characters.

The voice of compassion in 'Laxmi's Adventure'

After reading Manoj Das's stories, an extraordinary sense of compassion makes the reader's heart quiet. Such a great story is his 'The Dusky Horizon'. The story of 'Laxmi's Adventure' is not less compassionate. The events described in the story are brief. But he, who is a quiet reader, possessor of a calm heart, experienced and patient, shed tears not from his eyes but from the heart.

When a girl like Laxmi dies at an early age, there is no reader whose heart cannot be shaken by deep sorrow. The stream of tears that silently flow in the readers is not to be seen, but only to be felt. The death of a girl like Laxmi brings everyone into sorrow. Every reader feels as if his younger sister or his daughter has become soulless. Laxmi is the treasure of every reader's love and admiration. Despite being poor, she lives in an atmosphere of extraordinary love. If the wings of such a moving butterfly are broken, then who can stay in patience! After Laxmi's departure, we cannot imagine her parent's situation. Maybe that's why Manoj has restricted himself from drawing those tears. In the story 'The Dusky Horizon', the untimely death of the little girl makes her maternal grandfather soulless. The voice of prayer rose from the writer's heart- 'Such pain should never be felt again.' The readers may often feel that no one else in this world would suffer like Laxmi's parents.

The priest breaks the heart of Laxmi and later realises his rough behaviour. He dies soon after this realisation. Tears drop from the reader's eyes after seeing the transformation of this cruel heart. Man has the ability to forgive like God. Men are the children of God. So they have qualities like God. That is why the readers shed tears even at the death of the priest. These tears cannot not be seen by the empty eyes. These are very small. This can only be felt by someone who is very insightful, very empathetic and gentle.

The grief on the death of these two characters creates a deep sympathy in the reader's soul. There are so many tragic incidents in life that confuses human beings. Laxmi is very close to the readers. When the priest is repenting, he also wins the hearts and minds of the readers. He seems very close to the reader's heart. His death, though a revelation of the inner spirit, touches the heart of the readers so deeply that the readers weep inwardly. After reading the story the readers are left speechless for a long time. For a long time, they remained depressed and burned with pain. They have not the ability to respond or say something. By connecting two separate ideas in two characters, the pain that Manoj fills in the reader's soul will never fade away by time. That which fades away very quickly is called 'Watermark'. But when the mark that is drawn in the heart of the readers will never fade. Those who are connected with this story, know that there is an unextinguished lamp burning in the heart of this priest. The Priest's wish for death is his best wish. The best tribute is offered to him when the reader's hands are joined with tearful eyes. Manoj's portrayal of the character not only moistens the reader's soul with compassion, but the divine consciousness that exists within this compassion gives him strength and motivation.

Like 'Laxmi's Adventure', Fakir Mohan's 'Rebati', Kalindi Charan Panigrahi's 'Mansara Bilapa' and Laxmikant Mahapatra's 'Budha Shankhari', fill the reader's heart with tears. Those who are in search of happiness in life, can feel and understand the pain and tears that they get after reading these stories.

From this point of view, one can feel and understand the pain of the infinite stream of tears flowing in the story of 'Laxmi's Adventure'. One needs a little insight, a little sensitivity, a little sincerity in uniting the souls of Laxmi and the priest. Their eternal departure has a meaningful reality. It is a rare experience of being generous, selfless, pure and holy. 'Laxmi's Adventure' has given the readers that supernatural experience - this is a perfect relaxation. When such a supreme divinity emerges from within, then man becomes like a monk.

The Mysterious Secret of Child Psychology: 'Laxmi's Adventure'

Modern writers are always aware. The way that the human mind has been thoroughly analysed in psychology has had a profound effect on the short stories as well, which has already been exposed. Eminent critics have considered the significance of these stories and taken the readers to a higher level of human -consciousness. The way that the eminent psychologists of the world have explained the different levels of the human conscious, subconscious and unconscious mind, has become a different medium for the authors of the new inner consciousness. Whether it is the famous Sigmund Freud or Viktor Prankol - the way in which all of them have opened up the nature of the mind is a matter of attraction for writers. In the post-independence era, especially in the post-seventeenth stories, the stories which have been written by adopting this psychoanalytic style, have created mystery in the readers. So, an unpleasant truth needs to be told in this matter. That is, most of the psychological fiction that has been written has depicted the dark side of the human mind. Human beings look beautiful and honest on the outside. But all their lower instincts or passiveness of the soul are exposed in different ways. Such fictions have boldly portrayed the reality of human nature. The violent tendencies within humans, the darkness of pride, the passions, and the sexual urges that exist within them- all these are depicted in a very effective way. One can feel that this type of psychological study has not been particularly helpful in explaining the beauty of the human spirit. It must be worthless to say that such a psychological thought is the latest human related discovery. In this context, there is a need to take a new look at the story 'Laxmi's Adventure', which shows a new consciousness.

Literary critics who have noted the success of Manoj Das's children centric stories have found the scientific characterizations in his works, which are based on Western psychology. But can we look at the 'Laxmi's Adventure' story in a new way? There is no doubt that the real secret of this character Laxmi can be revealed without studying it from a psychological perspective.

Manoj Das presents small girls in his stories in a heart-warming way. From that point of view he is not only a literary sculptor or a fictionist, but rather a great psychologist. Without accepting any psychologist as his guide, he has assimilated the children's mind with deep selflessness. If we discuss the characteristics of Laxmi's character in this context, we can easily identify the uniqueness of Manoj's creation.

Laxmi is the main heroine in the story. In this story, Manoj has shown that it is not necessary to take the help of a psychologist to observe the emotions that arise in the mind of a little girl.

Laxmi is dreaming of God. For her, God is not a wooden statue or a stone statue without life. In the story 'Chalanti Thakur' by Shantanu Kumar Acharya, a child hides behind the old statue in a state museum. He utters the words, "I am not a dead God". It shakes the heart with extraordinary emotion.

Similarly, Laxmi thinks that God is her best friend. She feels that exchanging ideas with God is a normal process. Manoj has drawn our attention to the innovative direction of the study of the mind in writing this great truth. Laxmi's character is not just a girl who is saying nonsense words only. She is indeed a motherly figure who sees life very deeply above all these. Manoj has discovered the mother's love in every child. Within the psychoanalytical mode we can see how Laxmi is dreamlike, how she is close to God in the solitary environment during the day and finally she is frightened and dead.

The writer does not hesitate to express the simplicity of Laxmi's heart. She doesn't love falsehood, she doesn't love pretence. There is no doubt that she is a soft and sweet soul who is always devoted to God.

When a human child comes to this earth, he remains as the most sacred being. All the complexities of worldly life enter into him as he grows older. Manoj has highlighted this fact through his narration of another story. The name of the story is 'Krishna and Kansa'. It has been compiled in Manoj's book 'Kete Diganta'. Manoj Das has shown there that an artist has received the advice of God to draw the characters of 'Krishna and Kansa'. After that, he is in search of a model who is like the character of Krishna. He comes in contact with an eight-year-old boy who is playing near a river. That boy is innocent and intelligent. Thinking of him as his model and placing him in front of his eyes, he creates the most beautiful picture of Lord Krishna. After the completion of this painting, he cannot find a suitable cruel man, who will be fit for the Kansa model. Many years passed in between. Later he comes in contact with a criminal in prison who is suitable to be a model for Kansa. He brings that man to his house by the king's order. When he opens the previously drawn picture of Krishna in front of him, he sees tears in the eyes of that cruel man. He learns that he is the same person who was brought to the painter for the picture of Krishna when he was a boy of eight years old. The boy became a cruel and harsh criminal like Kansa after coming in contact with other criminals. This story conveys the great truth that the unique beauty of divinity exists within every child. Laxmi is a living embodiment of divinity in the story of 'Laxmi's Adventure'. In her, the author finds the pure simplicity, discovers a deep trust in God, and ultimately describes the unimaginable tolerance. Her love is very deep like the love of the parents for their children. She has the ability to give sympathy like parents. What does it mean? The meaning is the existence of the goddess within each child. Manoj has the ability to find divinity, which the modern psychologists fail to find. He has proved the divinity in man by creating the divine feeling and divine beauty in Laxmi. In addition to this, the priest's transformation which he presents also proves that the deepest truth of humanity is the eternal movement from darkness to light.

So the 'Laxmi's Adventure' story is not based on the theory of any psychologist. According to the analysis of the psychologists, it is possible to analyse the psychology of a man without looking at him, like Manoj Das has been able to portray in his story. In this context, Manoj's guide is not a psychologist. Rather, Manoj is the guide and best critic for psychologists. In this regard, Manoj's idea for the introduction of basic psychological research is an inspiration in the field of humanistic analysis. A great introduction to one of the best ideas. From that point of view, it is important to look at 'Laxmi's Adventure' story and the philosophy of Manoj's psychoanalysis from a new perspective.

The Experience of Laxmi

When the heroine travels to a fixed place for the purpose of meeting a handsome hero, she becomes his lover. We have read the poetry of Radha and Krishna's love. These writers have described Radha and Krishna's physical beauty and give such descriptions in the name of love that many readers have kept a distance from such love. In many stories the writers describe their passion by the name of love. Although this love is not merely a physical attraction, it is an intimate attraction of the soul to the divine. The readers have expressed their own concerns about the impact of these writings on society.

Can we imagine a different scenario in this context? The scene is like that Radha and Krishna have transformed into a little boy and a little girl and feel a deep attraction for each other. Does this scenario attack the evil mind of the readers? Radha and Krishna descended to this earth to consume love in the Reeti age. The union is not the sole ambition of their love. It is a hundred thousand times more important and innovative than this.

Laxmi sees God in her dream. The woman who can see her desired hero in her dreams, she is the real emotional heroine. Laxmi is filled with extraordinary thoughts. She is emotional and compassionate. If there is no connection by birth, it is not at all possible to dream of a divine and desirable hero. On the other hand, there are some heroes who have acquired the power to dream in others' minds. And God! He is Almighty. He will surely appear in the dream of the one, whom he wished to call to him with his wonderful love and affection. In the darkness, when you fall asleep with such a feeling, then the whole night is filled with love. Laxmi spent so many nights in confusion after looking at the beauty of God. She can understand the hint of her beloved God. That's why she waits for the sunrise every day. She Waits for the lonely environment at noon. It is only in the absence of the public that the relationship between the hero and the heroine is developed. Is it possible in the crowd, between the emotionless prayers of the devotees in the temple? That is why one who loves God never tries to get close to him with the noise of the crowd. One who is deeply in love with anyone, wants to meet him alone and be close to him. When a common man wants a crowded environment, lovers want emptiness and silence. Then it is a matter to think of the secret level that the Gods and Goddesses are communicating with each other. That is why there is a strong belief in the village - when the doors and gates close at night, the road becomes empty, then the Gods and Goddesses come out from the temple to walk. In the third hour of the night, when everyone is sleepy they talk to each other. Devotees who are blessed with heavenly peace sometimes hear the sweet melody in their ears. Sometimes the holy sound comes from their holy feet. It's not possible to see and even not everyone can hear it.

Laxmi is getting close to the heart of God in the lonely noon. In her heart there is boundless love, in her mind there are boundless emotions. There are countless thoughts in her heart. She waits for God to speak her heart when she gets close to him. Does Laxmi talk to God? Is there any excitement for mutual physical contact? Readers can feel the exchange of ideas in the distance. Those who have the lower sentimentality, they only speak about the lust in love. It lacks the deepest experience of unconditional love. What is Laxmi asking God? Is she praying for her own benefit? Nothing. She has nothing but the sentiments of her purest heart. Is it impossible for the readers to cry after knowing the union of God and Laxmi? The rare emotional sight of both of them is the best moment of life. If one can exchange thoughts with God for a moment, then it will be fruitful for his next billions of births. Man takes birth to gain this moment in life. We can't imagine how many births he spends to get this prolonged moment of joy. He doesn't want anything else after getting that. For that, Radha only wants to see Srikrishna's sweet face once from a distance. Sudama's life feels blessed with that love. With that love, Shabari's life is dedicated to Sriram. Dasia Bauri or Salabeg or Balaram Das - everyone's life has been filled with experiences of heavenly peace, love and joy. How could the life of our Goddess Laxmi not have been blessed by interacting with God !

Goddess Laxmi has appeared as a girl in this story. For this reason, the form of her love is not described. Her compassion is unimaginable. It is not possible for the common people like us to know the secret of the descendance and ascendance of God. Did Manoj think deeply to name the story as 'Laxmi's Adventure'? No, no, not that. The words spontaneously come to the writer's mind, like God and Goddess descend on earth. Can Manoj express the truth in front of common people like us about the wonderful joy he must have felt at the time of naming the story as 'Laxmi's Adventure'? On February 21, 1963, Manoj was able to see the form of Sri maa at Pondicherry, that mother is the heroine of this story named as Laxmi. Her presence is pure and holy. Her sentiments are far above worldly interests. Her charm is the effect of the flute that stirs in every blood cell. She is fully devoted. She has no dreams of her own. As soon as she sees God, her inner soul is shaken. The emotion of this pure and tearful self-surrender has given us the best meaning of love. We remained silent after knowing Laxmi's love. What else can we do but be silent? For the truth that Manoj has revealed in 'Laxmi's Adventure', we can offer our deepest gratitude in words. This is the heartily prayer to God that the nectar of Laxmi may fall on the powerless, desireless and thoughtless people like us.

The best story of Manoj Das

Manoj Das is a great bilingual writer. His esteemed readers have realised the respectable place he holds as a top novelist at the national and international level in Odisha and outside Odisha. Now Manoj is known for composing stories like 'Laxmi's Adventure'. He said that the inspiration with which he started writing the stories is currently unknown. That is why there is no doubt in Manoj's mind. This is because of this instinct he feels to write novels, travelogues and spiritual compositions. This is another unique expression of his creativity. Manoj has written so many influential short stories. Once he went on to highlight the reason in his composition, he said - a true identity of one's creative inner self can be found after composing at least half a dozen stories.

Manoj's novel has touched the peak of popularity. His 'Mystery of the Missing Cap', 'The Letter of the Last Spring', 'The Dusky Horizon', 'The Camel', 'A song for Sunday' and 'Laxmi's Adventure' have been awarded as his best stories. Manoj Das feels confused to answer about which is his best work when asked by the readers. At that time this story breaks his heart and he answers the question by naming the story 'Laxmi's Adventure'.

Manoj was at an immature age when he started

writing stories. At that time, by creating such brilliant stories, the love he spreaded in the readers was very heart touching. However, later he himself admitted that he could not properly express his genius when the story was written by him. The remarkable change in his consciousness and the way in which his hopeful future is revealed is his true identity. In this regard, if we think in a healthy mind, then we can definitely accept that the story 'Laxmi's Adventure' deserves the honour of being his best story. Manoj's faith and perspective of life are self-evident that it is his best story.

A literary writer can call his creation the best in which the truth of his philosophy of life has been effectively expressed. If the outline of Manoj's stories is squeezed, would not a reader feel that all of his themes are specifically found in the story of 'Laxmi's Adventure'? The tears and blood shed by Manoj are the most remarkable. While writing a story, it doesn't matter how a writer identifies his talent in different ways, rather the work in which the expression of his spirit shining as a lamp will be recognized as the best. When writers are asked about their best work, they usually give one answer. That is, all the creations are equally adorable to an artist like all the children are to a mother. It's the ultimate truth, but the children in whom ideal parents reflect the greatness of their hearts, don't they make them sit in the best place in their hearts? It is natural to have equal affection for all children. But the parents feel he is the best child who can sacrifice his life for the country. In this regard, we don't know Manoj's view on this, but he cannot deny that the reflection of his divine consciousness in the story of 'Laxmi's Adventure'. In this sense, the story is also the best symbol of a great inspiration for the readers, which touched their heart more than anything else. Who can deny that the vision of the great goal which Manoj has been idealised in the story is revealed in a different way? Franz Kafka, the eminent orator of the world, once said, 'Correcting oneself is more important than worshipping God.' The story 'Laxmi's Adventure' carries the message of that great worship. The widespread influence in terms of popularity has already been discussed. Sometimes the best writing is unable to gain popularity. But in the case of Manoj's story, which has gained great popularity, must also have achieved the value of the best story. If studied from different points of view, the best of this story is always represented in the heart.

Once a great literary artist of Odisha, who was very reluctant to accept the success of any other story except 'Laxmi's Adventure' while discussing the stories of Manoj Das. Knowing this, the pain that was created in the heart of this writer remains inexpressible. At that time, only he could feel the cry of his anguished soul. Today, after many years and the above mentioned great literary figure has passed away, the writer is in awe when he recalls his words. It's as if his heart is struggling with a different kind of idea. Interpreting the words of the scholar from a different perspective, he understands that Laxmi didn't actually come to Manoj's soul. Mahalaxmi is a compassionate character of Mahasaraswati and Mahakali. She came to give repentance to the cruel men of this earth. The story which moves from such a heavenly atmosphere centering on the celestial character radiates the highest quality. That great man could not easily acknowledge any other author, but acknowledged and congratulated Manoj's extraordinary achievement by calling this one story as his greatest creation. So the story's eternal meaning will be spread more when we discuss it more. Although the writer

Rabindranath Tagore wrote many stories, there is no doubt that 'Kabuliwala' is the manifestation of his best thought. Many writers of the world have created hundreds of stories, but the fame that they have earned for composing a single story is definitely memorable. From this point of view, when the story 'Laxmi's Adventure' is analysed like a piece of gold tested in a rough stone, this becomes brighter and brighter with its own unusual light. Divine power is auto generated – Manoj's well-published and well-loved writing is the best. No doubt, we feel the glory for it.

Two Glorious Forms of Divine Mother

That divine mother is Goddess Laxmi. In one form she appeared in Balaram Das's 'Laxmi Purana' and in another form, she became a light in Manoj Das's story 'Laxmi's Adventure'.

The popularity of 'Laxmi Purana' by Balaram Das, the great literary sage in the Panchasakha era, is a rare example in India. Who does not know the content in 'Laxmi Purana'! Goddess Laxmi comes out of the temple in the morning and enters the house of Sriya, who is a devotee. It surprises Sri Balabhadra and Sri Jagannath. There is no need to tell the story after that. The poet Balaram Das presents a great symbolic expression to attack casteism. His revolutionary value is eternal. Divine mother, without making any distinction between castes and religions, enters wherever she sees the spark of pure devotion. It indicates that wherever there is purity, and clarity of devotion - there descends Laxmi, the great Goddess of beauty. The story of Balabhadra and Jagannath is only meant to explain the ignorant people. In other words, if Lord opposes this greatness of Mahalaxmi, then he will be ever deprived by the offerings of Maa Laxmi. By composing such events, Balaram Das is trying to show that Lord himself is bound by the divine will of the divine mother. In this case, how can the common man escape from the divine mother's eyes?

Who is the little girl Laxmi in Manoj Das's story

'Laxmi's Adventure'? Maha Laxmi of 'Laxmi Purana' has appeared in the form of a little girl in this story. In the 'Laxmi Purana', where purity has appeared, Mother Laxmi has come there in glory. And here? Mother Laxmi enters the place where there is purity. In other words, the divine mother has entered the heart of an arrogant character like the priest and burned his heart with remorse. Here without any discrimination, wherever she sees the possibility of change, she enters into his innermost part with an incomparable love. Due to that reason, the priest is no longer the former priest. He has been transformed into a noble character who is repenting and whose later life indicates great possibility. It is absolutely impossible to be born speechless for the Priest, who prays to be born speechless. Because the tongue with which the priest uttered the evil words had been severed by the edge of the sword of his repentance. Is there any doubt in this world that he will be incarnated as a holy spirit after having experienced two births in one birth.

The story of Balaram Das's 'Laxmi Purana' must have influenced Manoj forever. How could he know that out of that desire, the pure hearted girl Laxmi would emerge like Maha Laxmi emerges from the churning of the ocean! Without telling anyone, Divine Mother herself descends like this into the calm heart of a literary writer. It is not possible for Balaram Das to compose this story in a planned way. Laxmi holds him in such an inspiring atmosphere where the inner eye of the poet is revealed. 'Laxmi Purana' is not just a fictional story. This is not only a conscious revolutionary step of the poet. This is an extraordinary landing of Mahalaxmi. Balaram Das is a holy medium of the beautiful and divine mother Mahalaxmi. Mahalaxmi enters into a man to give him such a revolutionary message in which she could see a tiny hole. Laxmi's entry into the heart of Balaram Das was arbitrary. Just like that in Manoj Das the divine mother has bestowed the grace to become a devoted writer. Therefore, even if a tiny particle of compassion that is expressed towards the priest touches the reader, which can lead to rebirth.

'Laxmi Purana' and 'Laxmi's Adventure' - both these works are inspired by the desire to bring human beings rebirth. Those who worship Laxmi only by respecting the traditions in the society and do not understand its meaning, their souls can never reach a higher level. Similarly, those who concentrate on 'Laxmi's Adventure' only for reading stories or for discussion, to them the real goal can never be achieved. 'Laxmi Purana' is not only a literary creation. In his view, 'Laxmi's Adventure' is not just the name of a story. This is an unique expression of divine mother's tender compassion. From that point of view, we have to give proper respect to both these literary creations, and our life can be filled with utmost love. Therefore, we can achieve the spiritual connection between these two works, if we can keep ourselves open to that rising moment of divine part.

Background

"What else is my rest? Writing is my rest" - this can only be said by those who consider literature as meditation. That evening, the author of this book Dr. Manindra Kumar Meher called out the story over the phone after returning from a distant college. He used to describe the character of Laxmi very heartily even in such a tired body. It seemed as if the writer's heart was saying that there is no hardship in the service of a mother. These are the words of Laxmi reflected from the heart of the divine mother. This resulted in beautiful stories which are in this book. While composing each story, all the fatigue of his body came down immediately, and a beautiful book is composed for the readers.

A book on the 'Laxmi's Adventure' story? - This is really a surprise for me. That day while discussing with Manindra Sir, he said that no matter how much one talks about the stories of Manoj Das, it is not enough for a critic. In fact, I feel the same in every article written by Manindra sir. Manoj Das has earned the reputation as a prominent writer not only in Odia literature but also in English literature because of his unique narrative style. The author of this book has realised that. Each story of Manoj Das is as entertaining as it is educational.

It is often observed that there are some stories that a reader thinks and reads again and again, the same condition is with Manindra Sir. Although every story is close to him, the joy he gets in 'Laxmi's Adventure' is expressed in every story of this book.

The readers who have read Manoj Das must have been overwhelmed with compassion after reading the story 'Laxmi's Adventure'. They must have felt that this Laxmi is no one else, a little girl whom you met recently. The inner words and feelings of a young girl that the writer has portrayed in this story are really unique. Along with this, the behaviour of the rural people, the behaviour of the men who claim to be the representative of God, the greed for money etc. are very successfully depicted in it. The author has discussed it in a very simple and gentle way.

I have felt that when Manindra sir pronounces the words for an article, he comes out of his own place to another state of consciousness. His eyes were looking at those scenes to create such stories. The way he told line after line without the slightest distraction, I felt like he was just uttering what some invisible force was telling him to write. In fact, that is the truth. The writer himself says that when he starts writing, an invisible force takes him to the end. And during the composition of this book, the Goddess Sri maa herself became the guiding force for him.

Each story included in this book is a discussion of different aspects of the story of 'Laxmi's Adventure'. The writer has revealed the real truth by comparing the artistic aspect of the story with the various writings of other writers, even with the best stories of Manoj Das. In each of the stories, the author has treated Laxmi as another form of Goddess Sri maa. Actually, that is the truth. As a mother tries to change the bad habits of a child without looking at his mistakes, similarly Laxmi is trying to change the priest and others in a silent way. The author very artistically depicts the way that God himself enters into the simple hearts of the children like Laxmi.

In this book, 'Laxmi's Adventure' story has been described by the author from two perspectives. One is the physical view and the another is the spiritual view. While explaining this aspect and in making the truth available to the readers, a true writer compares his text with other stories or other elements of the same story. Reading these stories will definitely take us to a different consciousness and make the truth accessible. Such as Laxmi with Reena in 'The Letter of the last spring', Laxmi with Sita in the story 'Groom for Sita', Laxmi with Rebati in 'Rebati', the Priest with Roy Babu in 'Teeth', 'Laxmi's Adventure' with 'Sarvabhuthesu' by Manoj Das. The way the author compares these characters as well as stories, the readers must have expanded the perspective from which they had previously viewed the story of 'Laxmi's Adventure'. The readers themselves can make available the importance of literature while comparing 'Laxmi's Adventure' with the stories of other countries. Not only stories, we can also notice that the characters are same in every section of literature and only physically different in this book. 'Gangadhar's Sita and Manoj's Laxmi' especially attract the heart from this aspect. In this story, the writer has successfully drawn Laxmi's heart with Sita in Ashoka forest.

Who is Savitri? She is Laxmi herself. She is Revati, Sita, Reena. The author has realised this. She is a little girl with a great soul. What will be her appearance? She spends just another day in another country or in another story. 'Laxmi is the conscious counterpart of Savitri', this book is particularly acceptable and educational from this point of view.

Manindra sir personally accepts that all the children are equal. Storytellers compose new stories just by changing their names. Laxmi, Rebati, Sita and Reena are the reflection of the heart of Sri maa herself.

The author himself feels that someone called out the words and lines when he composed this book, the reader may well realise it after reading it. It is absolutely true that the article which Manindra Sir starts without any preparation, is completed without any interruption. The energy he has gained to compose this book is actually the bliss of the divine mother. It's a matter of absolute joy that a book has been composed from a single story for the first time in Odia literature. There is no doubt that the readers of these stories will be united with the author's heart. In the author's opinion, even these stories are not enough for the story 'Laxmi's Adventure'. This story can be discussed from many more perspectives and new truths can be discovered.

The readers who have read Manoj's 'Laxmi's Adventure' previously, after reading this book, many new aspects will be revealed to them along with their previous experience. Their state of consciousness will be more expanded. Such a book can surely find a place in the heart of every reader as the best discussed book in our Odia literature.

Odia:

1. Das Manoj, *The Letter of the Last Spring.* First Edition, Vidyapuri, Cuttack-2, 1981

2. Das, Manoj, *Manoj Das nka katha o kahani,* Third Edition, Friends Publishers, Cuttack-2, 1981

3. Das Manoj, *Laxmi's Adventure,* Reprint, Grantha Mandir, Cuttack-2, 1987.

4. Das Manoj, *The Dusky Horizon and Other Stories.* Third Printing, Grantha Mandira, Cuttack-2, 1983

5. Das Manoj, *Shree Aurobindo* (Translation: Mahapatra Neelamani Sahu). Sahitya Academy, New Delhi, 1988.

6. Das Dasarathi, *Mahapatra Neelamani Sahoo nka Shrestha galpa,* First Edition, National Book Trust, India, New Delhi-70, 2014

7. Nanda Kumar Prema, *Maa* (Translation - Mahapatra Neelamani Sahu), National Book Trust India, New Delhi, 1977.

8. Sahu Mahapatra Neelamani, Sri Aurobindo's Epic, Savitri : A Study. Fourth Edition, Manorama Publishers, Balubazar, Cuttack-2, 2018.

9. Meher Gangadhar, Anthology of Swabhav Kavi Gangadhar (Editor - Dr. Manindra Kumar Meher). First Complete Edition, Grantha Mandir, Cuttack 2, 1998.

English:

1. Wilde Oscar, Complete Works of Oscar Wilde (Edited by J.B.-Foreman) Latest Reprint, Collins, London and Glasgow, 1976.

Black Eagle Books

www.blackeaglebooks.org
info@blackeaglebooks.org

Black Eagle Books, an independent publisher, was founded as a nonprofit organization in April, 2019. It is our mission to connect and engage the Indian diaspora and the world at large with the best of works of world literature published on a collaborative platform, with special emphasis on foregrounding Contemporary Classics and New Writing.

www.ingramcontent.com/pod-product-compliance
Lightning Source LLC
Chambersburg PA
CBHW020541080526
44583CB00013B/942